Holidays In Cross-Stitch
1990

The Vanessa-Ann Collection

The Vanessa-Ann Collection Staff

Owners:
Terrece Beesley Woodruff
and Jo Packham
Executive Editor:
Margaret Shields Marti
Editor:
Kristen Jarchow
Needlework Director:
Nancy Whitley
Graphic Artist:
Julie Truman
Graphing Director:
Susan Jorgensen
Operations Director:
Pamela Randall
Administrative Assistant:
Barbara Milburn
Customer Relations:
Gloria Baur

Designers

Trice Boerens
Dale Bryner
Treva Fendrick
Terry Johnson
Susan Jorgensen
Margaret Marti
Tina Richards
Julie Truman
Terrece Woodruff

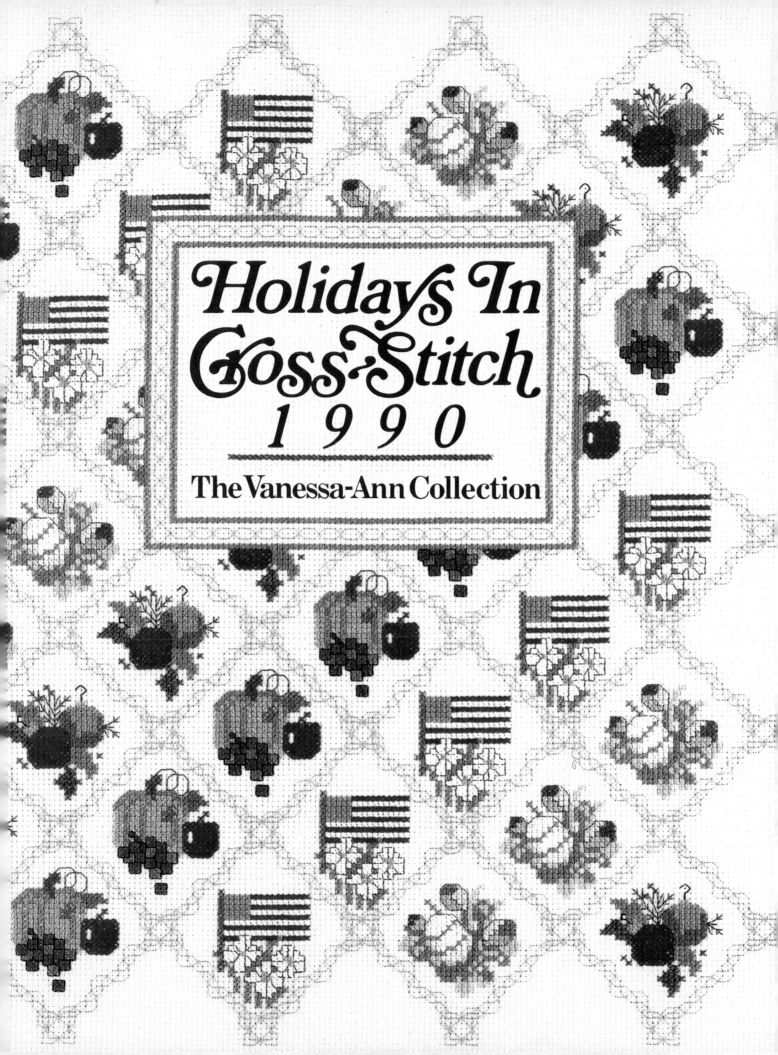

Holidays In Cross-Stitch 1990

The Vanessa-Ann Collection

To Lori, Lisa, and Shaun,
I continue to live for your joy-
ful noises—sometimes in har-
mony, sometimes not. Every day's
a new melody that enchants me as
each of you fine tunes your sym-
phony—or brass band, whichever
the case may be.
Love,
Mom

© 1989 by Oxmoor House, Inc.
Book Division of Southern Progress Corporation
P.O. Box 832463, Birmingham, Alabama 35201

Library of Congress Catalog Number: 86-62285
ISBN: 0-8487-0751-6
ISSN: 0890-8230
Manufactured in the United States of America
First Printing 1989

Executive Editor: Nancy Janice Fitzpatrick
Production Manager: Jerry Higdon
Associate Production Manager: Rick Litton
Art Director: Bob Nance

Holidays In Cross-Stitch 1990

Editor: Kim Eidson Crane
Editorial Assistant: Laurie Anne Pate
Production Assistant: Theresa L. Beste
Copy Chief: Mary Jean Haddin
Designer: Diana Smith Morrison
Artist: Denise Farmer Glenn
Photographers: Ryne Hazen

The Vanessa-Ann Collection wishes to thank the
following people for their trust and cooperation
during the photography for this book: Mary
Gaskill at Trends and Traditions; Boyd and Susan
Bingham; Hilltop Lanes; Susan Whitelock; Arnie
and Nan Smith; Courtney and Edie Stockstill;
Brigham Street Inn; and the Utah State
University Extension Farm.

To find out how you can order *Cooking Light*
magazine, write to *Cooking Light*®, P.O. Box
C-549, Birmingham, AL 35283

1 9 9 0
Contents

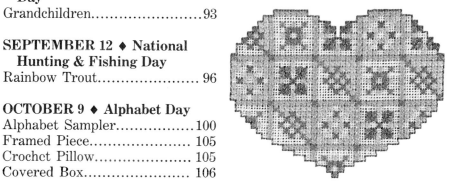

Introduction

In making something with our hands, we put our hearts into it as well. Each piece possesses a spirit that surfaces for the beholder to enjoy. The same is true in preparing each volume of *Holidays In Cross-Stitch*. The designers put their spirits into their work, drawing from their hearts as they prepare each piece.

When you complete one of our designs, you become part of this cycle of creativity. You leave your mark for all to remember and cherish. Make 1990 an even more memorable year for yourself and your loved ones with one of these cross-stitched designs.

1990

JANUARY
S	M	T	W	T	F	S
	1	2	3	4	5	6
7	8	9	10	11	12	13
14	15	16	17	18	19	20
21	22	23	24	25	26	27
28	29	30	31			

FEBRUARY
S	M	T	W	T	F	S
				1	2	3
4	5	6	7	8	9	10
11	12	13	14	15	16	17
18	19	20	21	22	23	24
25	26	27	28			

MARCH
S	M	T	W	T	F	S
				1	2	3
4	5	6	7	8	9	10
11	12	13	14	15	16	17
18	19	20	21	22	23	24
25	26	27	28	29	30	31

APRIL
S	M	T	W	T	F	S
1	2	3	4	5	6	7
8	9	10	11	12	13	14
15	16	17	18	19	20	21
22	23	24	25	26	27	28
29	30					

MAY
S	M	T	W	T	F	S
		1	2	3	4	5
6	7	8	9	10	11	12
13	14	15	16	17	18	19
20	21	22	23	24	25	26
27	28	29	30	31		

JUNE
S	M	T	W	T	F	S
					1	2
3	4	5	6	7	8	9
10	11	12	13	14	15	16
17	18	19	20	21	22	23
24	25	26	27	28	29	30

JULY
S	M	T	W	T	F	S
1	2	3	4	5	6	7
8	9	10	11	12	13	14
15	16	17	18	19	20	21
22	23	24	25	26	27	28
29	30	31				

AUGUST
S	M	T	W	T	F	S
		1	2	3	4	
5	6	7	8	9	10	11
12	13	14	15	16	17	18
19	20	21	22	23	24	25
26	27	28	29	30	31	

SEPTEMBER
S	M	T	W	T	F	S
						1
2	3	4	5	6	7	8
9	10	11	12	13	14	15
16	17	18	19	20	21	22
23	24	25	26	27	28	29
30						

OCTOBER
S	M	T	W	T	F	S
	1	2	3	4	5	6
7	8	9	10	11	12	13
14	15	16	17	18	19	20
21	22	23	24	25	26	27
28	29	30	31			

NOVEMBER
S	M	T	W	T	F	S
				1	2	3
4	5	6	7	8	9	10
11	12	13	14	15	16	17
18	19	20	21	22	23	24
25	26	27	28	29	30	

DECEMBER
S	M	T	W	T	F	S
						1
2	3	4	5	6	7	8
9	10	11	12	13	14	15
16	17	18	19	20	21	22
23	24	25	26	27	28	29
30	31					

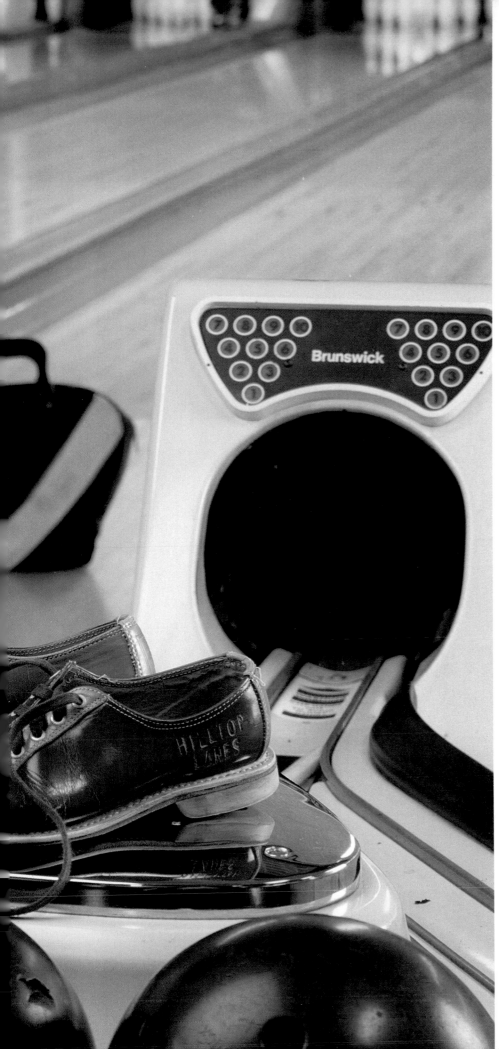

150th Anniversary of Bowling

Just imagine! For 150 years, bowling pins have been hit and missed in the pursuit of the perfect score. Since the first recorded tenpin match on New Year's Day, 1940, at Knickerbocker Alleys in New York City, the sport has become a national pastime.

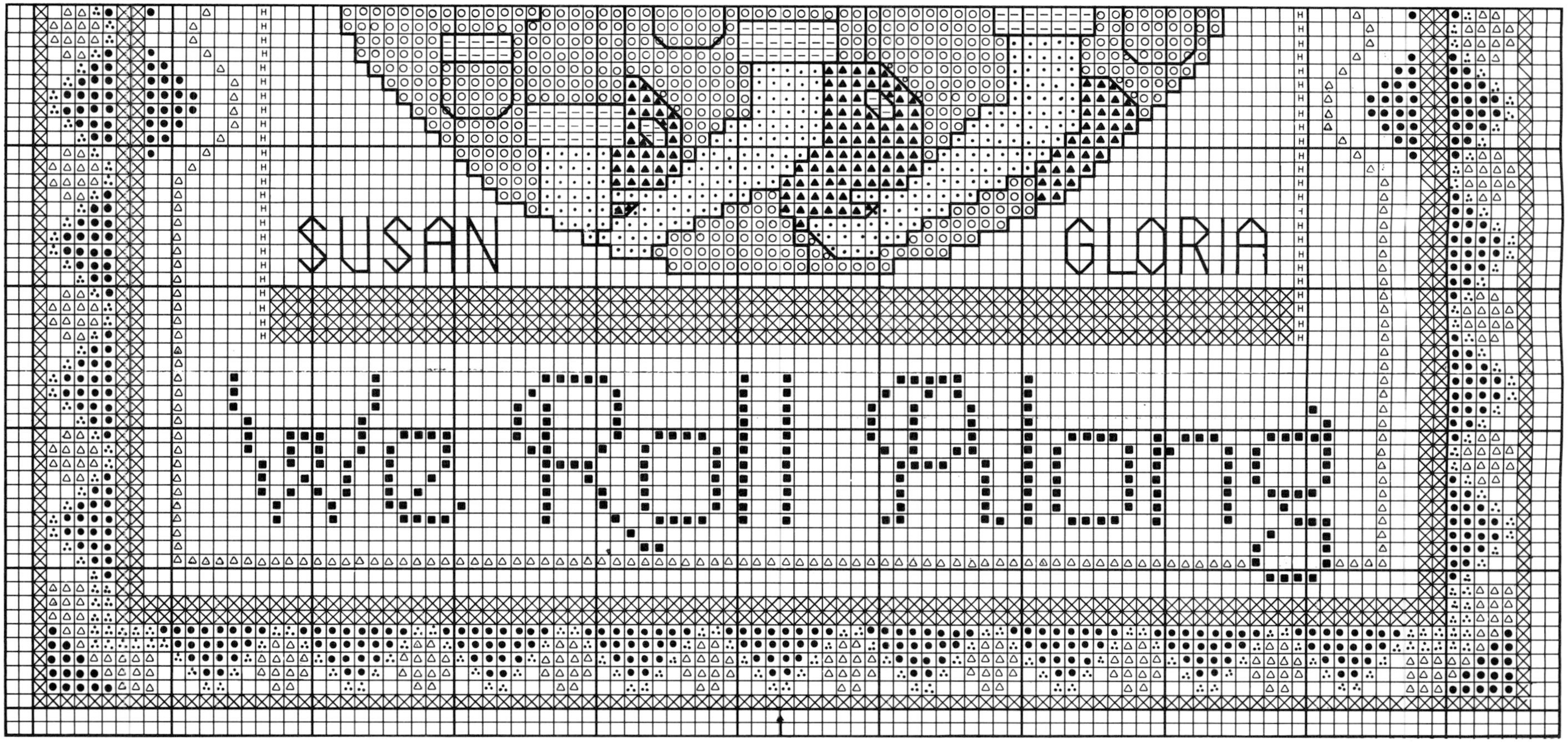

Stitch Count: 106 x 130

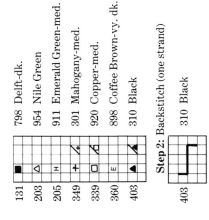

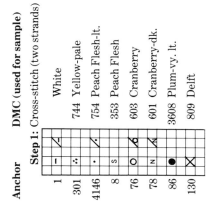

Tenpin Bowling Match

SAMPLE
Stitched on white Jobelan 28 over two threads, the finished design size is 7⅝" x 9¼". The fabric was cut 14" x 16".

Anchor			DMC (used for sample)
			Step 1: Cross-stitch (two strands)
1	–	⁄	White
301	∴		744 Yellow-pale
4146	·	⁄	754 Peach Flesh-lt.
8	S		353 Peach Flesh
76	O	⁄	603 Cranberry
78	N	⁄	601 Cranberry-dk.
86	●		3608 Plum-vy. lt.
130	X		809 Delft
131	■		798 Delft-dk.
203	△		954 Nile Green
205	H		911 Emerald Green-med.
349	+	⁄	301 Mahogany-med.
339	□	⁄	920 Copper-med.
360	E		898 Coffee Brown-vy. dk.
403	▲	⁄	310 Black
			Step 2: Backstitch (one strand)
403			310 Black

FABRICS
Aida 11
Aida 14
Aida 18
Hardanger 22

DESIGN SIZES
9⅝" x 11⅞"
7⅝" x 9¼"
5⅞" x 7¼"
4⅞" x 5⅞"

Lewis Carroll's Birthday

In 1862, C.L. Dodgson began telling a story about "Alice's adventures underground" to a favorite little girl named Alice Liddell and her sisters. Alice kept asking him to continue the story and by Christmas, 1864, he had written it out as a present for her. Under the pen name Lewis Carroll, he published *Alice's Adventures in Wonderland*, which has since been translated into more languages than almost any other work except the Bible.

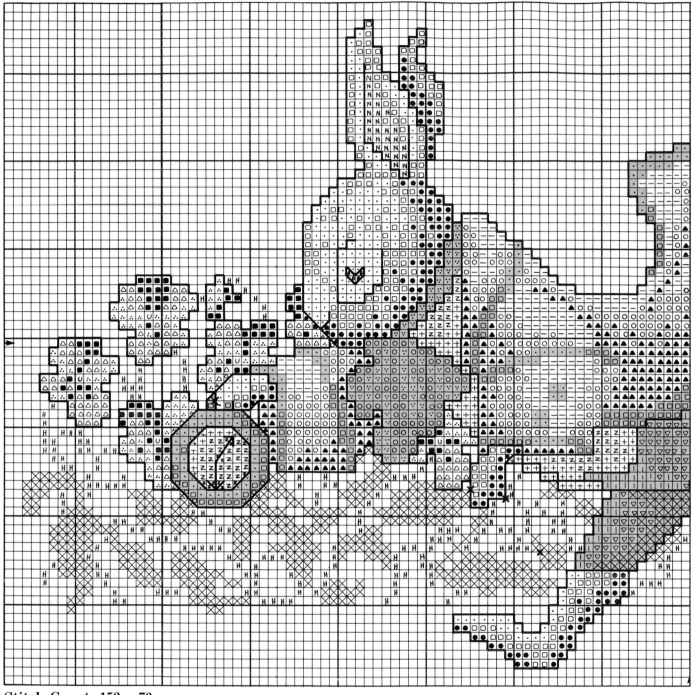

Stitch Count: 152 x 73

I'm Late! I'm Late!

SAMPLE
Stitched on white Belfast Linen 32 over two threads, the finished design size is 9½″ x 4½″. The fabric was cut 16″ x 11″.

Anchor			DMC (used for sample)
			Step 1: Cross-stitch (two strands)
1	Z		White
926	+	◹	Ecru
891	·	◹	676 Old Gold-lt.
890	▢	◹	729 Old Gold-med.
893	N		224 Shell Pink-lt.
42	◯		335 Rose

Anchor			DMC
59	⁙		326 Rose-vy. deep
104	△	◹	210 Lavender-med.
105	∴	◹	209 Lavender-dk.
118	■	◹	340 Blue Violet-med.
121	—		793 Cornflower Blue-med.
940	◯		792 Cornflower Blue-dk.
941	▲	◹	791 Cornflower Blue-vy. dk.
858	✕	◹	524 Fern Green-vy. lt.
859	H		522 Fern Green

14

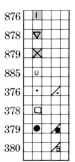

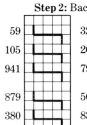

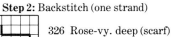

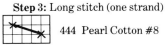

876	I	502 Blue Green
878	▽	501 Blue Green-dk.
879	X	500 Blue Green-vy. dk.
885	U	739 Tan-ultra vy. lt.
376	· ╱	842 Beige Brown-vy. lt.
378	□	841 Beige Brown-lt.
379	● ╱	840 Beige Brown-med.
380	╱B	839 Beige Brown-dk.

Step 2: Backstitch (one strand)

59	326 Rose-vy. deep (scarf)
105	209 Lavender-dk. (flowers)
941	791 Cornflower Blue-vy. dk. (jacket, vest)
879	500 Blue Green-vy. dk. (pants)
380	839 Beige Brown-dk. (all else)

Step 3: Long stitch (one strand)

444 Pearl Cotton #8

FABRICS
Aida 11
Aida 14
Aida 18
Hardanger 22

DESIGN SIZES
13⅞" x 6⅝"
10⅞" x 5¼"
8½" x 4"
6⅞" x 3⅜"

FEBRUARY 14
Valentine's Day

Exchanging gifts and greetings of love on Valentine's Day has been a custom since the 17th century. This special occasion gives us an opportunity to show our loved ones just how much we care.

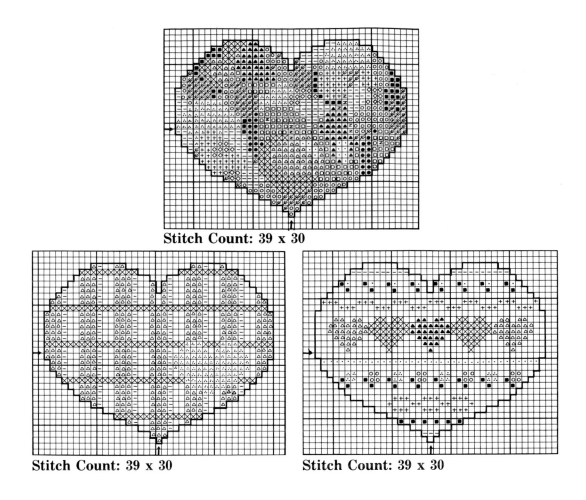

Stitch Count: 39 x 30

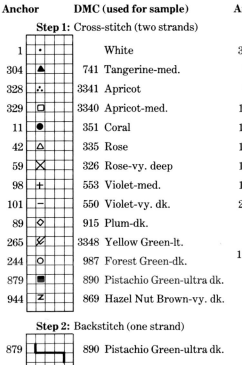

Stitch Count: 39 x 30

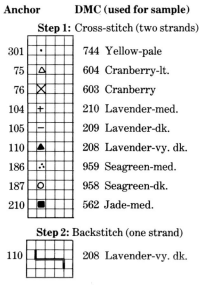

Stitch Count: 39 x 30

SAMPLES
Stitched on Belfast Linen 32 over two threads, finished design sizes are 2½″ x 1⅞″. Fabric was cut 7″ x 7″. For fancy stitches on ABC heart, see General Instructions.

Plaid Heart: Stitched on driftwood Belfast Linen 32.

Anchor		DMC (used for sample)	
Step 1: Cross-stitch (two strands)			
42	△	309	Rose-deep
42 121	✕	309	Rose-deep (1 strand) + 793 Cornflower Blue-med. (1 strand)
72	∴	902	Garnet-vy. dk.
378	−	841	Beige Brown-lt.

	Step 2: Backstitch (one strand)		
72		902	Garnet-vy. dk.

Fruit Heart: Stitched on white Belfast Linen 32.

Anchor		DMC (used for sample)	
Step 1: Cross-stitch (two strands)			
1	·		White
304	▲	741	Tangerine-med.
328	∴	3341	Apricot
329	□	3340	Apricot-med.
11	●	351	Coral
42	△	335	Rose
59	✕	326	Rose-vy. deep
98	+	553	Violet-med.
101	−	550	Violet-vy. dk.
89	◇	915	Plum-dk.
265	⊠	3348	Yellow Green-lt.
244	○	987	Forest Green-dk.
879	■	890	Pistachio Green-ultra dk.
944	Z	869	Hazel Nut Brown-vy. dk.

	Step 2: Backstitch (one strand)		
879		890	Pistachio Green-ultra dk.

Row of Hearts: Stitched on white Belfast Linen 32.

Anchor		DMC (used for sample)	
Step 1: Cross-stitch (two strands)			
301	·	744	Yellow-pale
75	△	604	Cranberry-lt.
76	✕	603	Cranberry
104	+	210	Lavender-med.
105	−	209	Lavender-dk.
110	▲	208	Lavender-vy. dk.
186	∴	959	Seagreen-med.
187	○	958	Seagreen-dk.
210	■	562	Jade-med.

	Step 2: Backstitch (one strand)		
110		208	Lavender-vy. dk.

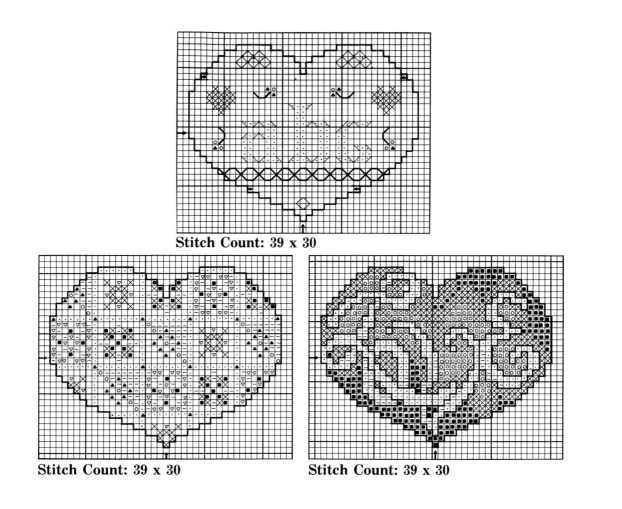

Stitch Count: 39 x 30

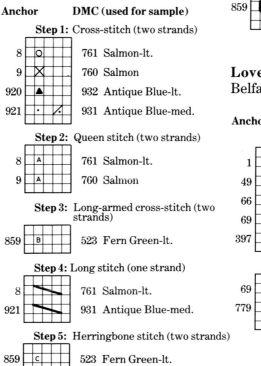

Stitch Count: 39 x 30

Stitch Count: 39 x 30

Quilt Squares Heart: Stitched on white Belfast Linen 32.

Anchor		DMC (used for sample)
		Step 1: Cross-stitch (two strands)
24	−	776 Pink-med.
27	O	899 Rose-med.
66	X	3688 Mauve-med.
128	▽	800 Delft-pale
121	▲	793 Cornflower Blue-med.
208	•	563 Jade-lt.
210	■	562 Jade-med.
		Step 2: Backstitch (one strand)
210		562 Jade-med.

ABC Heart: Stitched on cream Belfast Linen 32.

Anchor		DMC (used for sample)
		Step 1: Cross-stitch (two strands)
8	O	761 Salmon-lt.
9	X	760 Salmon
920	▲	932 Antique Blue-lt.
921	• /	931 Antique Blue-med.
		Step 2: Queen stitch (two strands)
8	A	761 Salmon-lt.
9	A	760 Salmon
		Step 3: Long-armed cross-stitch (two strands)
859	B	523 Fern Green-lt.
		Step 4: Long stitch (one strand)
8		761 Salmon-lt.
921		931 Antique Blue-med.
		Step 5: Herringbone stitch (two strands)
859	C	523 Fern Green-lt.

Step 6: Backstitch (one strand)

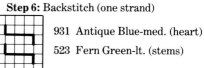

921		931 Antique Blue-med. (heart)
859		523 Fern Green-lt. (stems)

Love Heart: Stitched on white Belfast Linen 32.

Anchor		DMC (used for sample)
		Step 1: Cross-stitch (two strands)
1	•	White
49	O	3689 Mauve-lt.
66	X	3688 Mauve-med.
69	■	3687 Mauve
397	−	762 Pearl Gray-vy. lt.
		Step 2: Backstitch (one strand)
69		3687 Mauve (heart)
779		926 Slate Green-dk. (lettering)

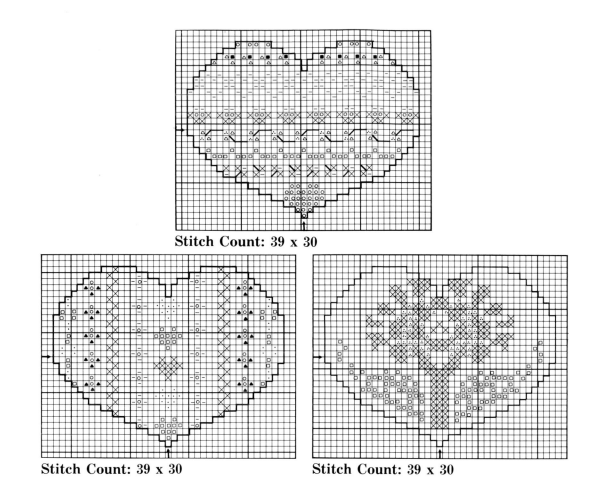

Stitch Count: 39 x 30

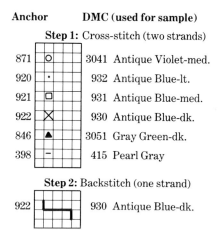

Stitch Count: 39 x 30

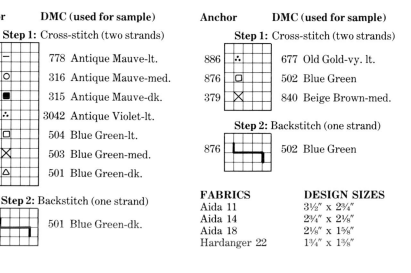

Stitch Count: 39 x 30

Blue Hearts: Stitched on cream Belfast Linen 32.

Anchor		DMC (used for sample)
		Step 1: Cross-stitch (two strands)
871	O	3041 Antique Violet-med.
920	•	932 Antique Blue-lt.
921	□	931 Antique Blue-med.
922	X	930 Antique Blue-dk.
846	▲	3051 Gray Green-dk.
398	–	415 Pearl Gray
		Step 2: Backstitch (one strand)
922		930 Antique Blue-dk.

Flowers Heart: Stitched on cream Belfast Linen 32.

Anchor		DMC (used for sample)
		Step 1: Cross-stitch (two strands)
968	–	778 Antique Mauve-lt.
969	O	316 Antique Mauve-med.
970	■	315 Antique Mauve-dk.
869	∴	3042 Antique Violet-lt.
213	□	504 Blue Green-lt.
875	X	503 Blue Green-med.
878	△	501 Blue Green-dk.
		Step 2: Backstitch (one strand)
878		501 Blue Green-dk.

Tree Heart: Stitched on driftwood Belfast Linen 32.

Anchor		DMC (used for sample)
		Step 1: Cross-stitch (two strands)
886	∴	677 Old Gold-vy. lt.
876	□	502 Blue Green
379	X	840 Beige Brown-med.
		Step 2: Backstitch (one strand)
876		502 Blue Green

FABRICS	DESIGN SIZES
Aida 11	3½" x 2¾"
Aida 14	2¾" x 2⅛"
Aida 18	2⅛" x 1⅝"
Hardanger 22	1¾" x 1⅜"

Fireplace Screen

MATERIALS

Completed cross-stitch for nine hearts
¼ yard of driftwood Belfast Linen 32; matching thread
Small pieces of cream and white Belfast Linen 32 for bottom border
One 17″ square of polyester fleece
Purchased fireplace screen

DIRECTIONS

All seam allowances are ¼″.

1. Cut each design piece 4½″ x 4½″ with the design centered. Designate Blocks 1-9 (Diagram A).

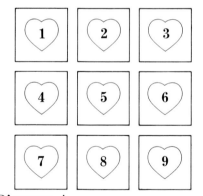

Diagram A
1. Love Heart
2. Blue Hearts
3. ABC Heart
4. Plaid Heart
5. Quilt Squares Heart
6. Tree Heart
7. Row of Hearts
8. Flowers Heart
9. Fruit Heart

2. From driftwood linen, cut the following pieces: three 5″ x 17″; four 1¼″ x 6½″; eight 1¼″ x 4½″; two 1¼″ x 5″; two 5″ x 6¼″. From cream linen, cut four 1¼″ x 5″ pieces. From white linen, cut one 1¼″ x 5″ piece.

3. Mark the center of one long edge of each 1¼″ x 6½″ strip and the center of each edge of Block 5. With right sides together, match centers of one strip and one edge of block. Stitch strip to within ¼″ of each corner of block; backstitch. Repeat with remaining strips.

4. To miter the corners of Block 5, fold the right sides of two adjacent strips together and stitch at a 45-degree angle (Diagram B). Trim seam allowance to ¼″ and press. Repeat for each corner.

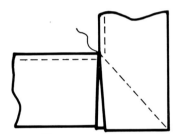

Diagram B

5. Stitch one 1¼″ x 4½″ piece to each of the tops and bottoms of Blocks 4 and 6. Then stitch Blocks 4, 5, and 6 together (Diagram C) to complete the center row.

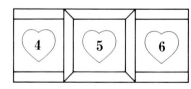

Diagram C

6. Construct top and bottom rows alike. Stitch one 1¼″ x 4½″ piece to each of the right and left edges of Blocks 2 and 8. Then join Blocks 1 and 3 to either side of Block 2 to complete top row; join Blocks 7 and 9 to either side of Block 8 to complete bottom row.

7. Stitch the long edges of the three rows together.

8. To prepare bottom border, stitch the long edges of the seven 1¼″ x 5″ strips together in this order: cream, driftwood, cream, white, cream, driftwood, cream. Stitch the two 5″ x 6¼″ pieces to each end as shown in Diagram D. This will be the bottom border piece.

9. Mark the center of one long edge of each border strip and the center of each long edge of the pieced center section. With right sides together, match centers of bottom border strip and bottom edge of center section. Stitch border to within ¼″ of each corner of the block; backstitch. Repeat with remaining border strips, trimming outside edges to make even.

10. To miter corners, repeat Step 4. For complete piece, see Diagram D.

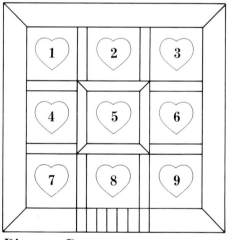

Diagram D

11. Place one layer of fleece behind completed piece. Insert in fireplace screen, following the manufacturer's directions.

Love Makes the World Go Round

SAMPLE

Stitched on cream Linda 27 over two threads, the finished design size is 8⅛″ x 8¼″. The fabric was cut 12″ x 11″.

MATERIALS

Completed cross-stitch on cream Linda 27
Small amount of blue/pink fabric; matching thread
⅛ yard of 45″-wide cream/pink fabric
½ yard of 45″-wide lilac print fabric for border and back
Small amount of lavender pindot fabric
Small amount of tan/red stripe fabric
1 yard of ¼″-wide blue satin ribbon
1⅝ yards of 1″-wide purchased lilac bias tape; matching thread
Ten ⅜″ bright pink heart buttons; matching thread
Two ½″ purple bird buttons
One 12″ x 16″ piece of polyester fleece
Dressmakers' pen

DIRECTIONS

All seam allowances are ¼″.

1. Cut Linda 10½″ x 9″ with design centered. From blue/pink print, cut two 1″ x 10½″ strips. From cream/pink fabric, cut two 2½″ x 10½″ strips. From lilac print, cut one 12″ x 15½″ piece for the back; two 1¼″ x 13″ strips and two 1¼″ x 16¼″ strips for the border.

2. With right sides together, pin the long edges of one blue/pink print strip to one cream/pink print strip. Repeat with remaining blue/pink and cream/pink strips. With right sides together, pin the blue/pink print to the top edge of the design piece and stitch. Repeat at the bottom of the design piece.

3. To attach the lilac print border, match the center of one short strip to the center of top cream/pink strip and pin, right sides together. Stitch to within ¼″ of corners; backstitch. Repeat with the second short strip on the bottom edge. Repeat to attach the 15¾″ lilac strips to the sides of the hanging.

4. To miter the corners, fold the right sides of two adjacent border strips together and stitch at a 45° angle (Diagram A). Trim the seam allowance to ¼″.

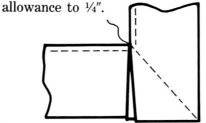

Diagram A

5. To make hearts, cut 2″-wide strips of lavender pindot to equal 20″. Also cut 1″-wide strips of tan/red stripe to equal 20″. Stitch long edges of the two pieces, with right sides together. Trace and cut out the heart pattern. Place heart pattern on the stitched strips, matching line on pattern to seam in the fabric (Diagram B). Cut out ten hearts. Mark the placement for the first heart in the horizontal center

of the top cream/pink section with the top of the heart ½″ below the lavender print border. Then mark the placement for remaining hearts on either side, ⅛″ apart. Repeat on bottom cream/pink section with the tip of the heart ½″ above the border. Appliqué hearts.

6. Layer backing, right side down, fleece, and top, right side up. Baste.

7. Using blue thread, quilt around heart block in center of design section; just inside border around trees, quilting across corners on the diagonal and around the children, following their general shape. Mark lines around design to make a square, ¼″ from tops of children's heads. Mark another square 1″ outside that. (The wording will be centered within this border. See photo.) Quilt on marked lines. Also quilt around appliquéd hearts and inside all straight seams.

8. Cut ribbon into two equal lengths. Lay ribbon ¼″ inside lilac borders on long sides of hanging. Attach by quilting down both edges of ribbon through all layers.

9. Sew one heart button to center top of each heart. Sew one bird button to each upper corner of quilting lines around words.

10. Bind edges with purchased bias tape.

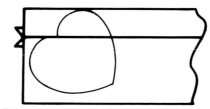

Diagram B

Pattern

Stitch Count: 110 x 112

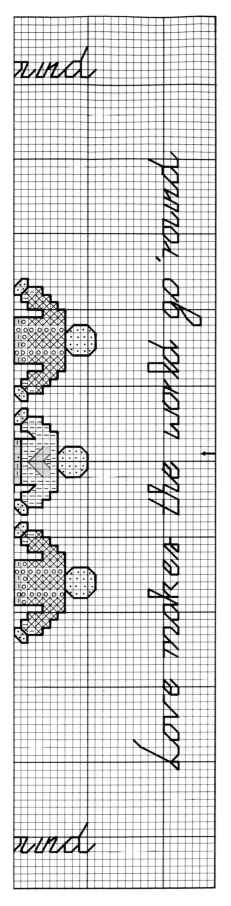

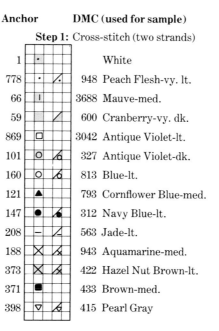

Anchor			DMC (used for sample)
Step 1: Cross-stitch (two strands)			
1	·		White
778	·	╱	948 Peach Flesh-vy. lt.
66	I		3688 Mauve-med.
59		╱	600 Cranberry-vy. dk.
869	□		3042 Antique Violet-lt.
101	○	╱	327 Antique Violet-dk.
160	○	╱	813 Blue-lt.
121	▲		793 Cornflower Blue-med.
147	●	╱	312 Navy Blue-lt.
208	−	╱	563 Jade-lt.
188	✕	╱	943 Aquamarine-med.
373	✕	╱	422 Hazel Nut Brown-lt.
371	■		433 Brown-med.
398	▽	╱	415 Pearl Gray

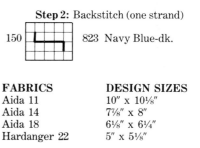

Step 2: Backstitch (one strand)

150   823 Navy Blue-dk.

FABRICS	DESIGN SIZES
Aida 11	10" x 10⅛"
Aida 14	7⅞" x 8"
Aida 18	6⅛" x 6¼"
Hardanger 22	5" x 5⅛"

Battles of the Flowers

Flowers are a cherished commodity in the south of France, where they are grown to make perfume. Their importance is recognized in the Battles of the Flowers, which take place in Nice. The 12 days of festivities include a parade in which all the floats are made of flowers. Battles ensue when, at a signal, fairgoers begin throwing flowers at each other. This amicable conflict always has the same outcome—lots of smiles and lots of flowers!

Floral Bouquet

SAMPLE

Stitched on cream Belfast Linen 32 over two threads, the finished design size is 7½" x 7½". The fabric was cut 13½" x 13½".

FABRICS	DESIGN SIZES
Aida 11	10⅞" x 10⅞"
Aida 14	8½" x 8½"
Aida 18	6⅝" x 6⅝"
Hardanger 22	5⅜" x 5⅜"

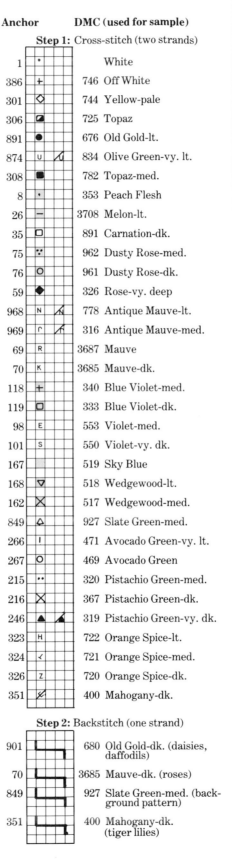

Anchor			DMC	(used for sample)
			Step 1:	Cross-stitch (two strands)
1	•			White
386	+		746	Off White
301	◇		744	Yellow-pale
306	◪		725	Topaz
891	●		676	Old Gold-lt.
874	U	◿	834	Olive Green-vy. lt.
308	◼		782	Topaz-med.
8	∙		353	Peach Flesh
26	−		3708	Melon-lt.
35	◻		891	Carnation-dk.
75	⁚		962	Dusty Rose-med.
76	O		961	Dusty Rose-dk.
59	◆		326	Rose-vy. deep
968	N	◺	778	Antique Mauve-lt.
969	⌐	◿	316	Antique Mauve-med.
69	R		3687	Mauve
70	K		3685	Mauve-dk.
118	+		340	Blue Violet-med.
119	◻		333	Blue Violet-dk.
98	E		553	Violet-med.
101	S		550	Violet-vy. dk.
167			519	Sky Blue
168	▽		518	Wedgewood-lt.
162	✕		517	Wedgewood-med.
849	△		927	Slate Green-med.
266	I		471	Avocado Green-vy. lt.
267	O		469	Avocado Green
215	••		320	Pistachio Green-med.
216	✕		367	Pistachio Green-dk.
246	▲	◤	319	Pistachio Green-vy. dk.
323	H		722	Orange Spice-lt.
324	<		721	Orange Spice-med.
326	Z		720	Orange Spice-dk.
351	◿		400	Mahogany-dk.

			Step 2:	Backstitch (one strand)
901			680	Old Gold-dk. (daisies, daffodils)
70			3685	Mauve-dk. (roses)
849			927	Slate Green-med. (background pattern)
351			400	Mahogany-dk. (tiger lilies)

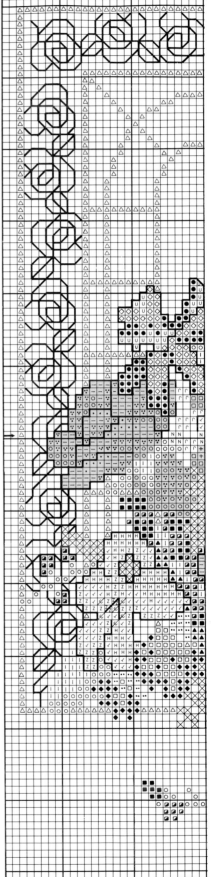

Stitch Count: 119 x 119

MARCH 17
St. Patrick's Day

The Claddagh, two hands holding a heart, is an Irish symbol for love and friendship. The more familiar shamrock is a symbol for good fortune. Stitch one of these emblems as a St. Patrick's Day gift and make someone's Irish eyes smile!

Claddagh

SAMPLE

Stitched on white Belfast Linen 32 over two threads, finished design size is 2½" x 2¼". Fabric was cut 8" x 8". See Suppliers for information on ordering porcelain jars.

Anchor			DMC (used for sample)	

Step 1: Cross-stitch (two strands)

886	·	∕	677	Old Gold-vy. lt.
891	△	◿	676	Old Gold-lt.
881	–	◿	945	Sportsman Flesh
159	O	◢	3325	Baby Blue
145	▲	◤	334	Baby Blue-med.
214	▢		368	Pistachio Green-lt.
257	✕	◿	3346	Hunter Green
268	●	◤	3345	Hunter Green-dk.

Step 2: Backstitch (one strand)

147		312	Navy Blue-lt. (cuffs and sleeves)
268		3345	Hunter Green-dk. (stems)
309		435	Brown-vy. lt. (crown and hands)

FABRICS	DESIGN SIZES
Aida 11	3½" x 3¼"
Aida 14	2¾" x 2⅝"
Aida 18	2⅛" x 2"
Hardanger 22	1¾" x 1⅝"

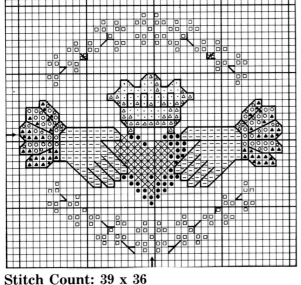

Stitch Count: 39 x 36

Locket

SAMPLE

Stitched on white Belfast Linen 32 over one thread, the finished design size is 1¼" x 1⅛". The fabric was cut 3" x 3". See Suppliers for information on ordering lockets.

Anchor		DMC (used for sample)	

Step 1: Cross-stitch (one strand)

257	O	3346	Hunter Green
268	▲	3345	Hunter Green-dk.

Step 2: Backstitch (one strand)

268		3345	Hunter Green-dk.

FABRICS	DESIGN SIZES
Aida 11	1⅛" x 1½"
Aida 14	⅞" x 1⅛"
Aida 18	¾" x ⅞"
Hardanger 22	⅝" x ¾"

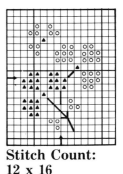

Stitch Count: 12 x 16

MARCH 21
Agriculture Day

Whether your kind of agriculture is potted plants and leafing through seed catalogs or the kind that involves rows of corn in wide open spaces, this day marks the beginning of the growing season. Vegetable gardeners and wheat farmers alike sow their seeds and look forward on this day to a season of bountiful harvests.

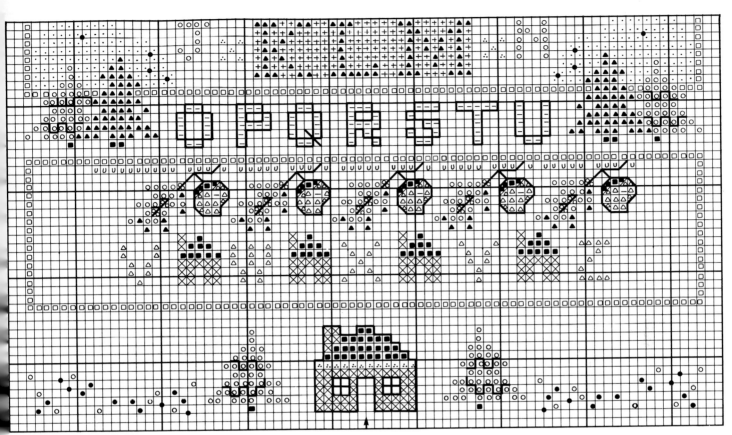

Stitch Count: 80 x 144

Farm Life Sampler

SAMPLE
Stitched on driftwood Belfast Linen 32 over two threads, the finished design size is 5″ x 9″. The fabric was cut 11″ x 15″.

Anchor		DMC (used for sample)
	Step 1:	Cross-stitch (two strands)
886	·	677 Old Gold-vy. lt.
891	–	676 Old Gold-lt.
323	U	722 Orange Spice-lt.
324	E	721 Orange Spice-med.
42	●	309 Rose-deep
969	+	316 Antique Mauve-med.
970	∴	315 Antique Mauve-dk.
920	X	932 Antique Blue-lt.
921	N	931 Antique Blue-med.
214	□	368 Pistachio Green-lt.
216	○	367 Pistachio Green-dk.
879	▲	890 Pistachio Green-ultra dk.
309	△ ◢	435 Brown-vy. lt.
380	■ ◤	839 Beige Brown-dk.

Step 2: Backstitch (one strand)

970		315 Antique Mauve-dk. (in letter A)
879		890 Pistachio Green-ultra dk. (grass borderline, apple stems)
380		839 Beige Brown-dk. (all else)

Step 3: French Knots (one strand)

879	●	890 Pistachio Green-ultra dk.

FABRICS	DESIGN SIZES
Aida 11	7¼″ x 13⅛″
Aida 14	5¾″ x 10¼″
Aida 18	4½″ x 8″
Hardanger 22	3⅝″ x 6½″

APRIL 1
April Fool's Day

Until the 16th century, the new year began on March 25. People would celebrate with eight days of festivities that ended on April 1. As European countries started adopting January 1 as the beginning of the year, those people who refused to give up the old custom were called April fools. This jester is an elegant reminder of the holiday's origin.

Jester

SAMPLE
Stitched on brown Perforated Paper 14, the finished design size for the arms is 3⅛" x 3⅞"; the body is 5½" x 9"; the legs are 2⅞" x 4¾". Use one 12" x 18" sheet of paper. The double lines on the graphs for the arms and legs indicate the cutting lines.

MATERIALS
Completed cross-stitch on brown
  Perforated Paper 14
¾ yard of ¼"-wide red/gold braid
¼ yard of ½"-wide gold picot
  braid
One gold tassel
Four ¼"-wide antique glass buttons; matching thread

DIRECTIONS
1. On the perforated paper of each arm and leg piece, mark very lightly with a pencil where the double lines occur on the graph. Carefully cut one hole outside the pencil lines and design area, rounding out curves of some areas. Cut one hole outside the jester's head and body.

2. Glue the red/gold braid on the red cross-stitch on the front and bottom edges of the coat, using one continuous piece for the left side, around the back of neck, and down the right side to the scarf. Place the second piece of braid just below the scarf, gluing it down the right front and across the right side. Glue pieces of the braid along bottom of each sleeve cuff.

Glue the gold picot braid to the wrong side of the coat bottom, to extend from the lower edge. Glue the tassel to the center top of the hat.

3. Match the M symbol on the arm front to the back of the jacket shoulder. Sew a button loosely but securely through both layers of paper. Repeat to attach the other arm and the legs.

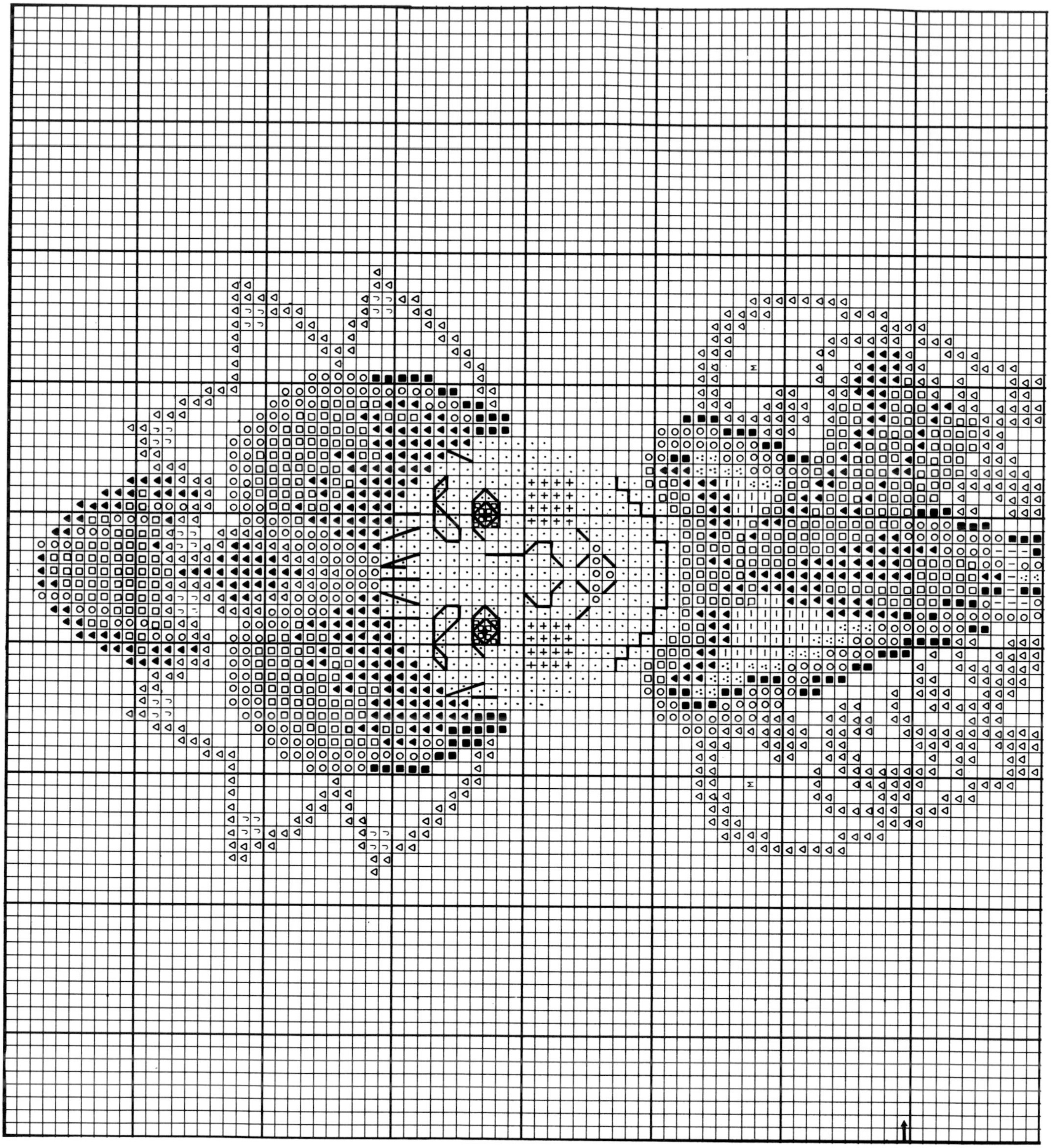

Stitch Count: 83 x 135

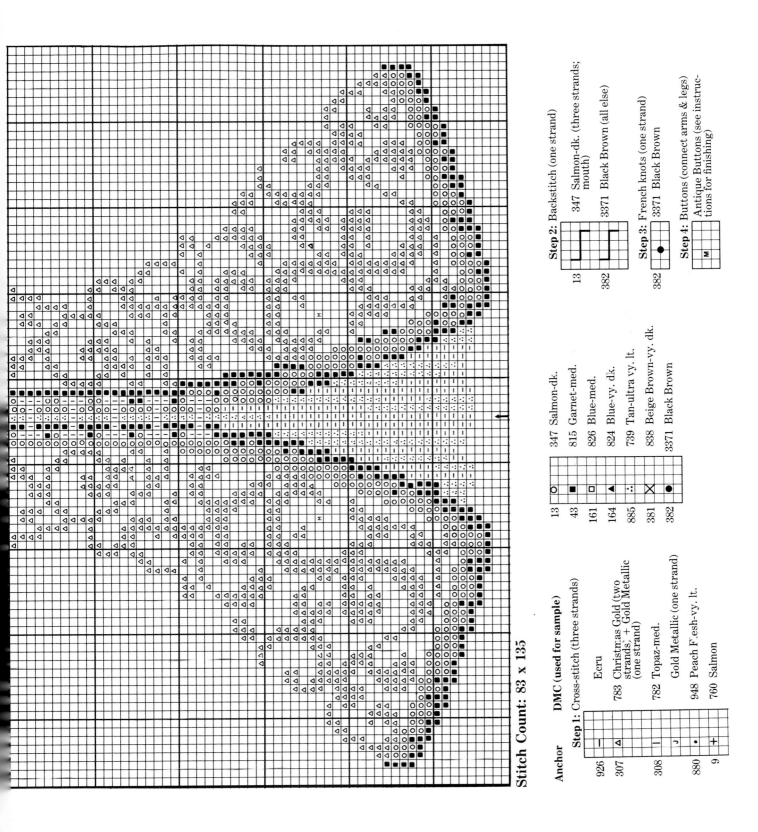

Anchor	DMC (used for sample)

Step 1: Cross-stitch (three strands)

926	—	Ecru
307	◁	783 Christmas Gold (two strands) + Gold Metallic (one strand)
308	⌐	782 Topaz-med.
		Gold Metallic (one strand)
880	•	948 Peach Flesh-vy. lt.
9	+	760 Salmon
13	○	347 Salmon-dk.
43	■	815 Garnet-med.
161	□	826 Blue-med.
164	◀	824 Blue-vy. dk.
885	∴	739 Tan-ultra vy. lt.
381	✕	838 Beige Brown-vy. dk.
382	●	3371 Black Brown

Step 2: Backstitch (one strand)

| 13 | | 347 Salmon-dk. (three strands; mouth) |
| 382 | | 3371 Black Brown (all else) |

Step 3: French knots (one strand)

| 382 | ● | 3371 Black Brown |

Step 4: Buttons (connect arms & legs)

| M | | Antique Buttons (see instructions for finishing) |

39

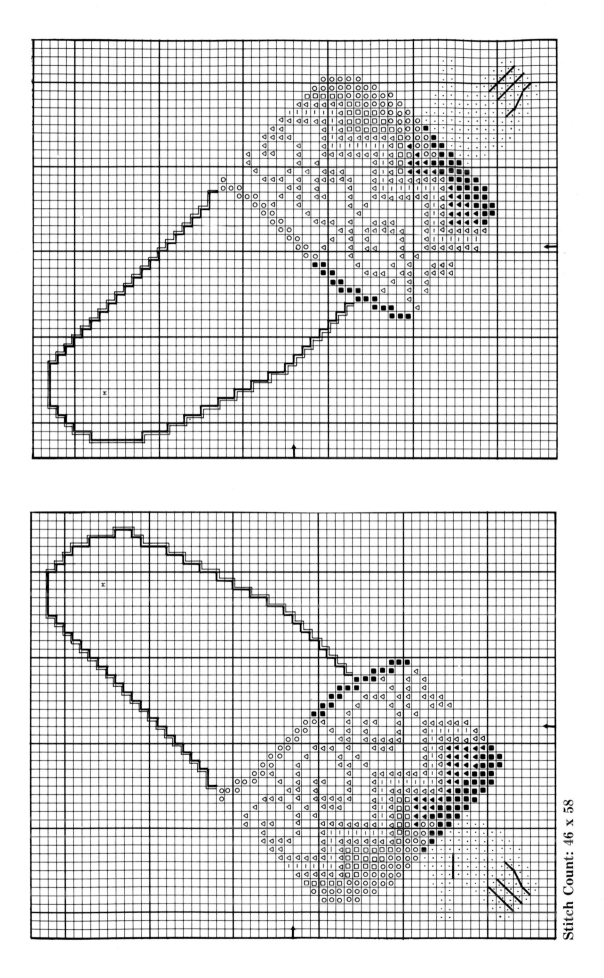

Stitch Count: 46 x 58

40

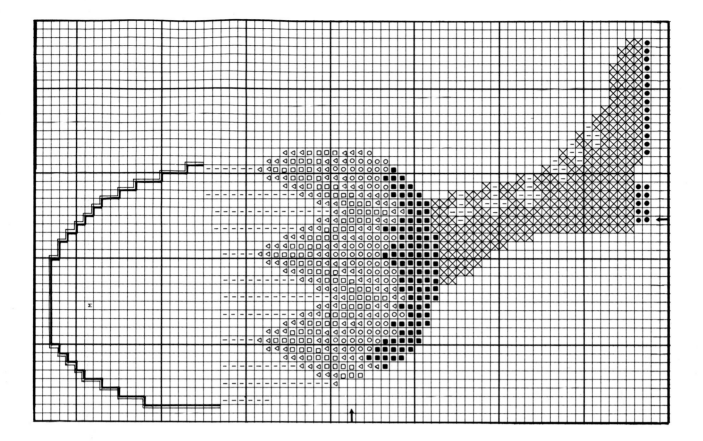

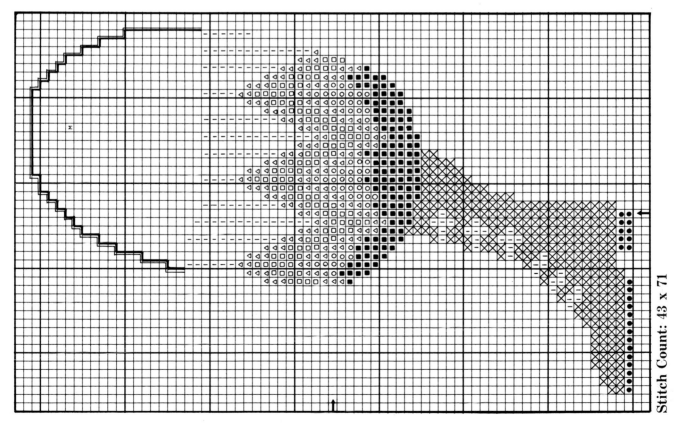

APRIL 10
Passover

This holiday begins an eight-day celebration of the Jewish Festival of Freedom. Today, to celebrate, Jewish families eat a ceremonial dinner called a Seder, at which they retell the story of the Exodus, the escape of the Jews from slavery. Blessings and songs also celebrate this day of freedom.

Passover Tablecloth

SAMPLE
Stitched on white Belfast Linen 32 over two threads, the finished design size is 6¼" x 6¼". The fabric was cut 10" x 10". Repeat design three times for tablecloth shown in photo.

MATERIALS
1¼ yards of white Belfast Linen 32 (includes fabric for three design squares and 16 unstitched squares for tablecloth); matching thread

7 yards of ⅛"-wide double-edged lace trim

5¼ yards of 2"-wide lace trim

DIRECTIONS
Note: Directions are for a 28½" x 64" tablecloth. The size of the tablecloth may be altered by adding or subtracting 8" squares.

1. With the design centered, trim the three stitched pieces to 8" squares. To prevent the fabric from fraying, zigzag the edges. Cut sixteen 8" squares from the unstitched linen. Zigzag all edges.

2. To join the squares, cut sixteen 8½" pieces of double-edged lace. To make the center row of the tablecloth, lay one edge of a lace piece along the top edge of one design piece. Using a narrow zigzag stitch, attach the lace to the linen. Then zigzag the opposite edge of the lace to an unstitched square of linen. Continue zigzagging lace to unstitched squares to make a row of one design square followed by six unstitched squares. Trim the ends of the lace so that they are even with edges of squares. Repeat for the two side

rows, joining squares with double-edged lace, except only five unstitched squares will follow the design square.

3. To join the three rows, cut two 52" pieces of double-edged lace. Following the procedure in Step 2, zigzag one long edge of lace to the edge of the six unstitched squares in the center row. (Do not attach this lace to the design square.) Then zigzag the opposite edge of the lace to a side row including the design square. Repeat with the remaining side row (Diagram A).

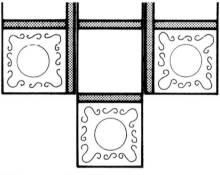

Diagram A

4. Zigzag the 2"-wide lace to all outside edges of tablecloth. To miter the corners, fold the right sides of two adjacent pieces of lace together and stitch at a 45° angle (Diagram B). Trim the seam allowance to ⅛". Zigzag over the mitered seam to finish.

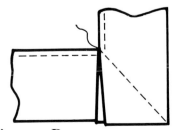

Diagram B

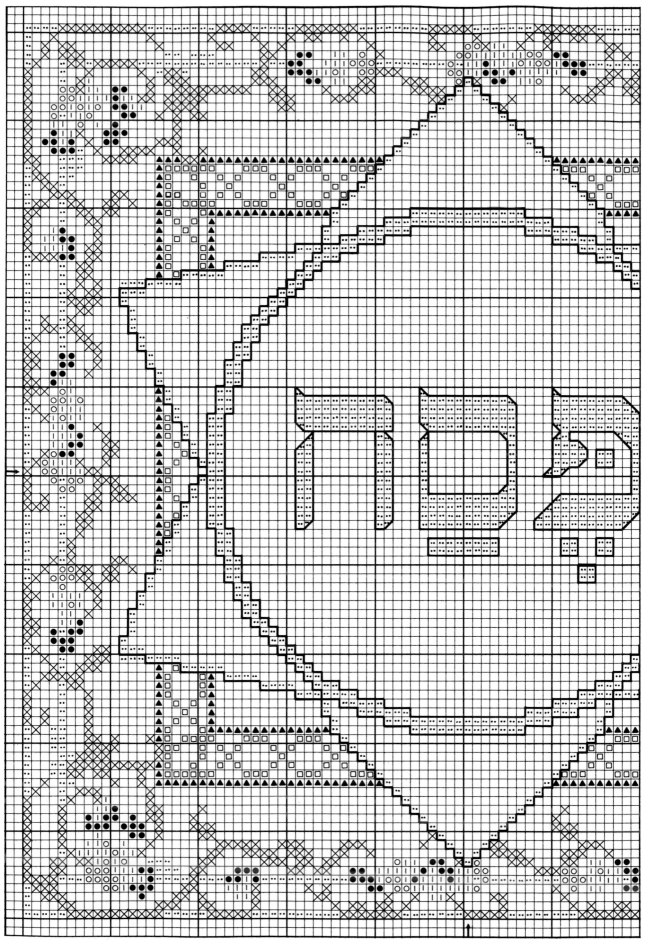

Stitch Count: 101 x 101

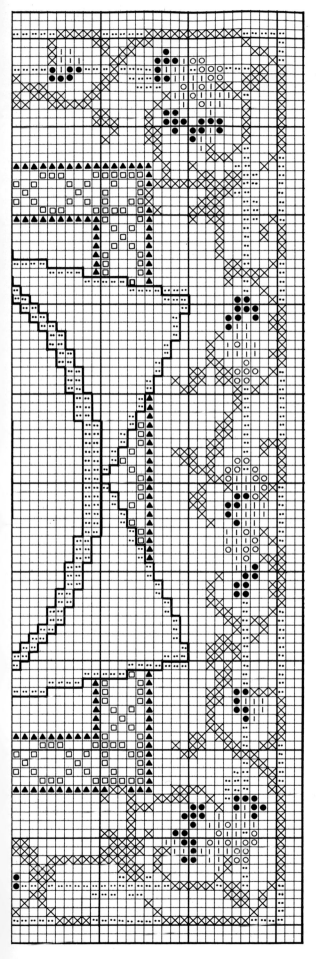

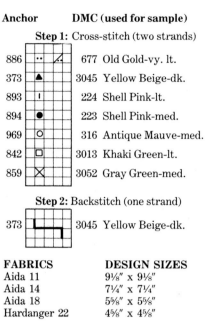

Anchor　　　**DMC (used for sample)**

Step 1: Cross-stitch (two strands)

Anchor		DMC	
886	·· ╱	677	Old Gold-vy. lt.
373	▲	3045	Yellow Beige-dk.
893	ı	224	Shell Pink-lt.
894	●	223	Shell Pink-med.
969	○	316	Antique Mauve-med.
842	□	3013	Khaki Green-lt.
859	✕	3052	Gray Green-med.

Step 2: Backstitch (one strand)

373	⌐	3045	Yellow Beige-dk.

FABRICS　　　**DESIGN SIZES**
Aida 11　　　　　9⅛" x 9⅛"
Aida 14　　　　　7¼" x 7¼"
Aida 18　　　　　5⅝" x 5⅝"
Hardanger 22　　4⅝" x 4⅝"

APRIL 15
Easter

Easter is a time for rejoicing. It is a time to marvel at the beauties of spring and the miracles of rebirth. Young and old enjoy the traditions of this joyous holiday. Take time this season to brighten your home with one of these Easter projects!

Easter Pillow

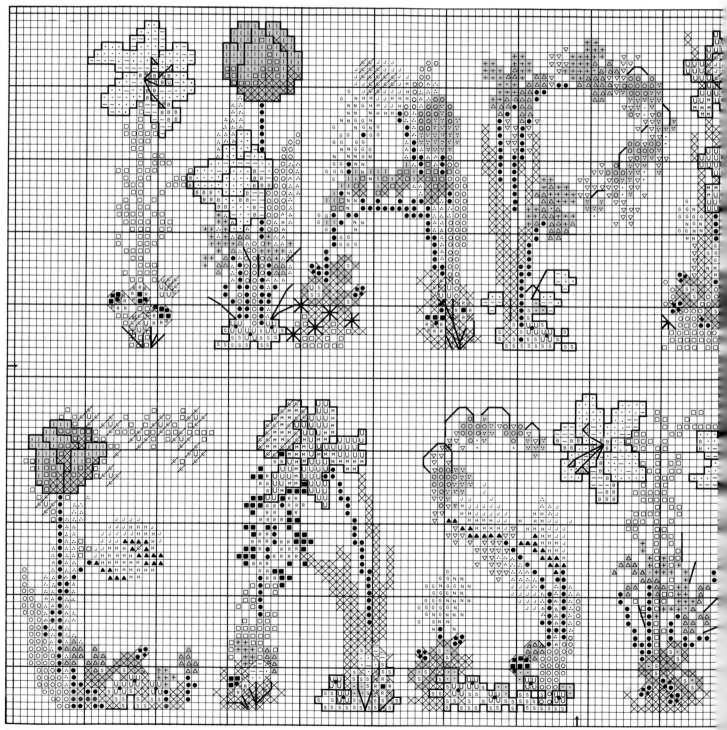

Stitch Count: 155 x 95

48

SAMPLE

Stitched on moss Lugana 25 over two threads, the finished design size is 12⅜″ x 7⅝″. The fabric was cut 20″ x 14″.

FABRICS	DESIGN SIZES
Aida 11	14⅛″ x 8⅝″
Aida 14	11⅛″ x 6¾″
Aida 18	8⅝″ x 5¼″
Hardanger 22	7″ x 4⅜″

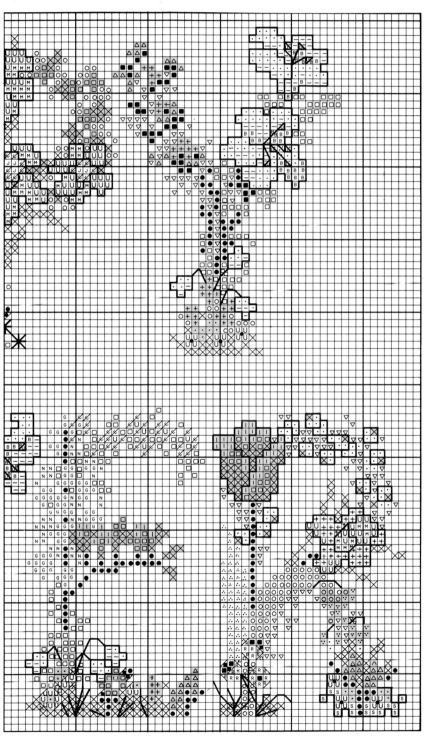

Anchor			DMC (used for sample)
Step 1: Cross-stitch (two strands)			
1	·	⁄	White
386	+	⁄	746 Off White
301	U	⁄	744 Yellow-pale
303	·	⁄	742 Tangerine-lt.
891	M	M	676 Old Gold-lt.
329	⁄	⁄	3340 Apricot-med.
25	I		3708 Melon-lt.
26	□		894 Carnation-vy. lt.
35	H		891 Carnation-dk.
35 / 329	J		891 Carnation-dk. (one strand) + 3340 Apricot-med. (one strand)
59	▲		326 Rose-vy. deep
76	✕		603 Cranberry
85	G		3609 Plum-ultra lt.
88	+		718 Plum
69	O		3687 Mauve
70	∴		3685 Mauve-dk.
95	N		554 Violet-lt.
98	△	◿	553 Violet-med.
117	R	R	341 Blue Violet-lt.
119	■	◢	333 Blue Violet-dk.
900	—	⁄	928 Slate Green-lt.
849	B		927 Slate Green-med.
265	S	◿	3348 Yellow Green-lt.
266	◻	◿	3347 Yellow Green-med.
216	✕	⁄	367 Pistachio Green-dk.
209	O	◿	913 Nile Green-med.
228	∴		910 Emerald Green-dk.
187	▽		992 Aquamarine
189	●	◿	991 Aquamarine-dk.
Step 2: Backstitch (one strand)			
901			680 Old Gold-dk. (daffodils)
69			3687 Mauve (tulips)
921			931 Antique Blue-med. (lilies, sweet peas)
216			367 Pistachio Green-dk. (all else)
Step 3: Smyrna cross (one strand)			
921	✳		931 Antique Blue-med.
Step 4: French knots (one strand)			
216	●		367 Pistachio Green-dk.

MATERIALS

Completed cross-stitch on moss
  Lugana 25; matching thread
⅓ yard of unstitched moss Lugana 25 for pillow backing
1¼ yards of print fabric
4 yards of medium cording
Stuffing

DIRECTIONS

All seam allowances are ¼".

1. With the design centered, cut
the Lugana 17" x 13". From remaining Lugana, cut a 17" x 13"
piece for the pillow back.

2. To make corded piping, cut a
1"-wide bias strip from print fabric, piecing as needed, to make 4
yards. Cut a 60" piece of bias strip.
Cut a 60" piece of cording, place it
in the center of the wrong side of
the bias strip, and fold the fabric
over the cording. Using a zipper
foot, stitch close to the cording
through both layers of fabric. Trim
the seam allowance ¼" from the
stitching line. With right sides together and raw edges aligned,
stitch the piping to the design
piece.

3. To make covered cording for
loops, cut a 35" piece from the bias
strip. Fold strip, with right sides
together, to measure ½" wide.
Stitch, leaving ends open for turning. Turn right side out. Thread
34" of cording through the casing.
Fold the ends in ½" and slipstitch
closed. In same manner, make four
12" pieces of covered cording. Set
aside.

4. With right sides together,
stitch design piece to pillow back,
stitching on the stitching line of
the piping and leaving an opening
for turning. Clip corners and turn
right side out.

5. To make loops on top edge of
pillow, find the center of the 34"
piece of covered cording. Make a
2½" loop. Slipstitch loop to the center top of the pillow. Working to
the right, make three more loops
of decreasing size, ending 5½"
from the corner. Slipstitch in
place. Repeat with loops on left
side.

6. Stuff pillow. Slipstitch the
opening closed.

7. For corner bow, use one of the
12" pieces of covered cording.
Make 1½" loops (see Diagram).
Tack loops securely. Repeat to
make three more bows. Slipstitch
a bow to each corner.

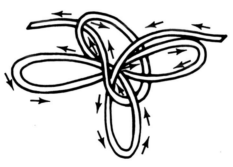

Diagram

Calico Rabbit

SAMPLE

The design was stitched on pistachio Aida 14. The finished design
size for the body is 7⅝" x 7⅜"; one
ear is 1¼" x 3⅛". The fabric was
cut 12" x 12" for the body and 3" x
6" for each ear.

MATERIALS

Completed cross-stitch on pistachio Aida 14
One 9" x 10" and two 3" x 5"
  pieces of unstitched pistachio
  Aida for the back; matching
  thread
⅜ yard of ⅜"-wide pink gros-
  grain ribbon
Stuffing
Dressmakers' pen
Tracing paper for patterns

DIRECTIONS

All seam allowances are ¼".

1. Trace and cut out the patterns
for the body and the ear. Center
the patterns on the stitched designs and trace one body and two
ears. Cut out. Also cut one body
and two ears from the unstitched
Aida.

2. Place the right sides of one
stitched and one unstitched ear
piece together. Stitch the edges,
leaving the bottom edge open. Clip
the tip and turn. Repeat for the
other ear.

3. Fold a ¼"-deep tuck in the
open edge of each ear. Pin the
front of the ears to the right side of
the body front, with raw edges
aligned and ear tips down.

4. Place the right sides of the body front and back together. Stitch, leaving an opening at the bottom for turning. Clip the curved seam allowances on each side, especially between the arm and leg. Turn the body right side out and stuff firmly. Slipstitch the opening closed.

5. Tie the ribbon around the rabbit's neck. Trim the ends.

Body

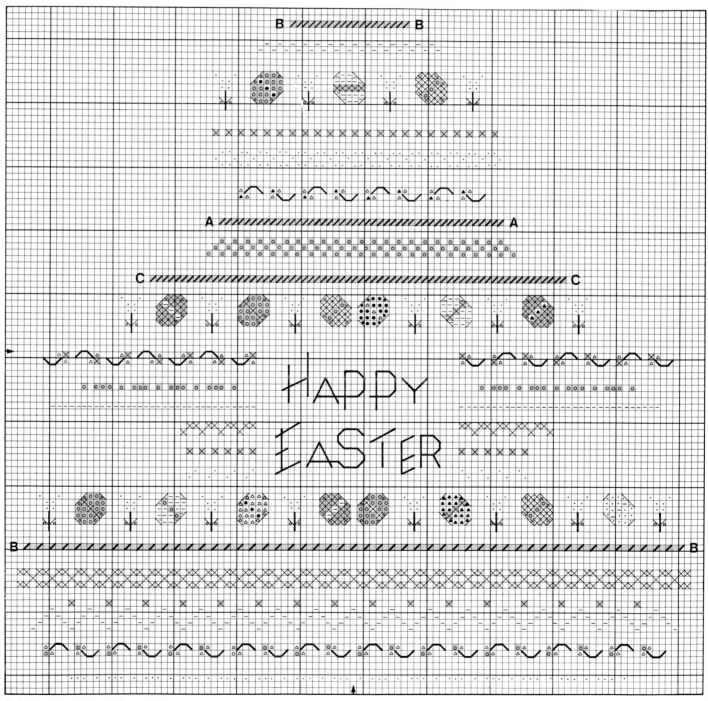

Stitch Count: 107 x 104

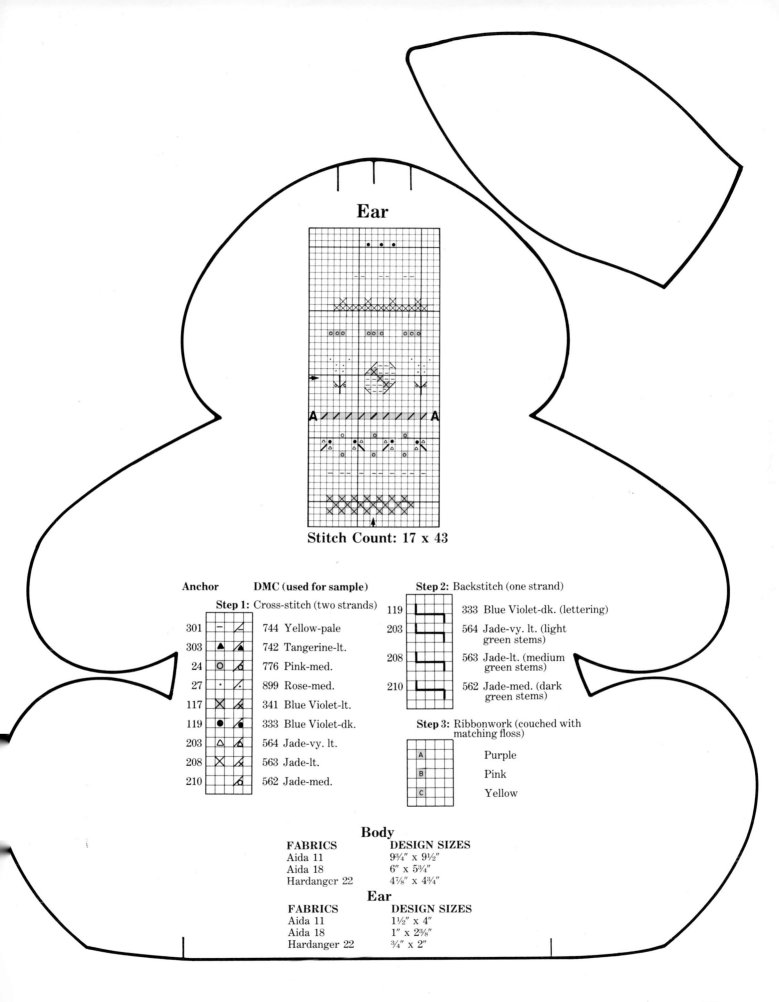

Ear

Stitch Count: 17 x 43

Anchor			DMC (used for sample)
Step 1: Cross-stitch (two strands)			
301	–	⁄	744 Yellow-pale
303	▲	◢	742 Tangerine-lt.
24	○	◢	776 Pink-med.
27	·	⁄	899 Rose-med.
117	✕	⁄	341 Blue Violet-lt.
119	●	◢	333 Blue Violet-dk.
203	△	◢	564 Jade-vy. lt.
208	✕	◢	563 Jade-lt.
210		◢	562 Jade-med.

Step 2: Backstitch (one strand)

119		333 Blue Violet-dk. (lettering)
203		564 Jade-vy. lt. (light green stems)
208		563 Jade-lt. (medium green stems)
210		562 Jade-med. (dark green stems)

Step 3: Ribbonwork (couched with matching floss)

A	Purple
B	Pink
C	Yellow

Body

FABRICS	DESIGN SIZES
Aida 11	9¾″ x 9½″
Aida 18	6″ x 5¾″
Hardanger 22	4⅞″ x 4¾″

Ear

FABRICS	DESIGN SIZES
Aida 11	1½″ x 4″
Aida 18	1″ x 2⅜″
Hardanger 22	¾″ x 2″

Easter Ornaments

SAMPLE
Stitched on white Linda 27 over two threads, the finished design size for the bird design is 8⅜″ x 1⅜″; for the rabbit design, 9⅛″ x 1¼″. The fabric was cut 12″ x 4″ for both.

MATERIALS (for one ball)
Completed cross-stitch on white Linda 27
One 3″ Styrofoam ball
One ball of Susan Bates/Anchor yarn: #8 (blue #0043), or Susan Bates/Anchor #8 (pink #4093), or DMC Cebelia #20 (yellow #745)
Size #10 steel crochet hook

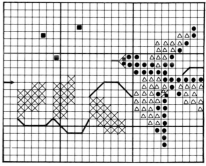

Stitch Count: 112 x 18

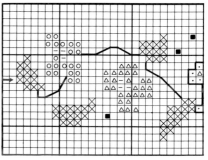

Stitch Count: 124 x 17

DIRECTIONS

All seam allowances are ¼″.

1. Trim the Linda to measure 1¾″ x 10″, with design centered. Stitch short ends together. Machine-stitch close to both long edges. Fold under ⅛″ on each long edge.

2. Crochet the top and bottom of the ornament:

Round 1: Working over the folded edge in rounds, work 84 single crochet stitches around one edge.

Round 2: * Single crochet in each of next 6 stitches, work a decrease over the next 2 stitches as follows: (insert hook in next stitch, pull up a loop) twice, yarn over, pull through all 3 loops on hook, repeat from * around until a total of 12 rounds have been worked, work a slipstitch in the last 3 stitches to end. Do not fasten off, chain 50, single crochet in same stitch as beginning to make a hanger, turn, work 50 single crochet stitches over the chain loop, slipstitch in beginning stitch. Fasten off. Repeat Round 1 on other edge of design strip. Insert Styrofoam ball. Repeat Round 2, omitting the hanger loop.

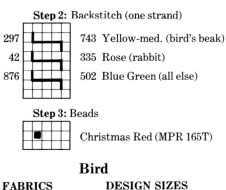

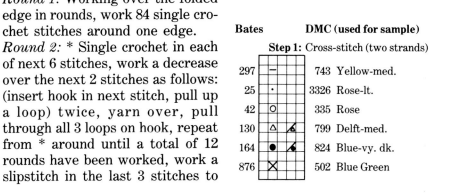

Bates **DMC (used for sample)**

Step 1: Cross-stitch (two strands)

Bates	Symbol		DMC
297	—		743 Yellow-med.
25	·		3326 Rose-lt.
42	O		335 Rose
130	△	◢	799 Delft-med.
164	●	◢	824 Blue-vy. dk.
876	✕		502 Blue Green

Step 2: Backstitch (one strand)

Bates	DMC
297	743 Yellow-med. (bird's beak)
42	335 Rose (rabbit)
876	502 Blue Green (all else)

Step 3: Beads

Symbol	
■	Christmas Red (MPR 165T)

Bird

FABRICS	DESIGN SIZES
Aida 11	10⅛″ x 1⅝″
Aida 14	8″ x 1¼″
Aida 18	6¼″x 1″
Hardanger 22	5⅛″ x ⅞″

Rabbit

FABRICS	DESIGN SIZES
Aida 11	11¼″ x 1½″
Aida 14	8⅞″ x 1¼″
Aida 18	6⅞″ x 1″
Hardanger 22	5⅝″ x ¾″

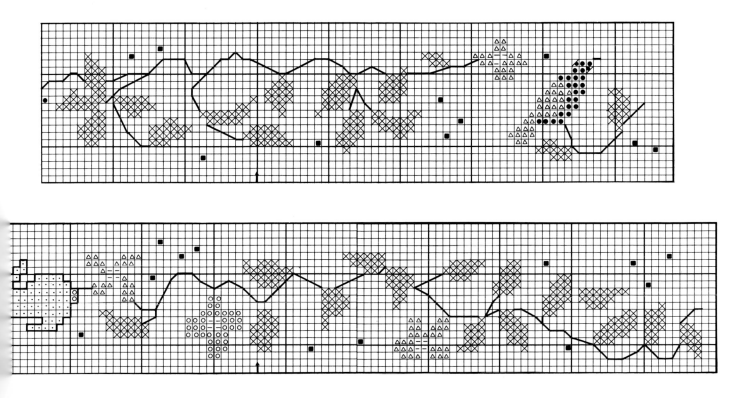

MAY 1
Mother Goose Day

What child doesn't delight in the promise of a story? Even adults feel a twinge of longing at the thought of curling up, cuddled and loved, for a story-telling session. Reread a favorite childhood nursery rhyme to experience again the warmth of Mother Goose's embrace.

Stitch Count: 121 x 121

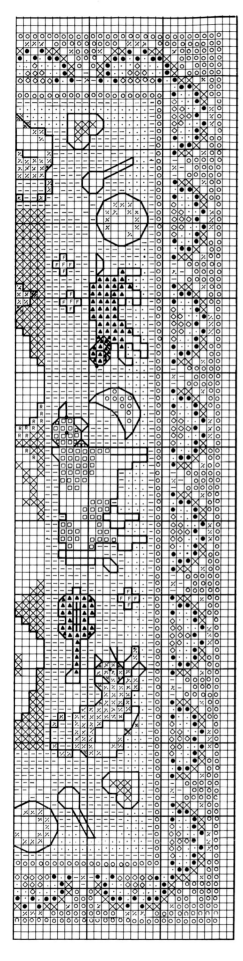

Mother Goose

SAMPLE

Stitched on white Jobelan 28 over two threads, the finished design size is 8⅝″ x 8⅝″. Fabric was cut 15″ x 15″. Also needed: 9″ of ⅛″-wide light blue silk ribbon for bow.

Anchor			DMC (used for sample)
Step 1: Cross-stitch (two strands)			
292	∴		3078 Golden Yellow-vy. lt.
886	O		677 Old Gold-vy. lt.
891	F		676 Old Gold lt.
892	I	╱	819 Baby Pink-lt.
892	△	◹	225 Shell Pink-vy. lt.
893	–	◿	224 Shell Pink-lt.
894	⊡		223 Shell Pink-med.
42			3350 Dusty Rose-vy. dk. (one strand) +
74	╱	◿	3354 Dusty Rose-lt. (one strand)
42	■	◿	3350 Dusty Rose-vy. dk.
869	R		3042 Antique Violet-lt.
118	◩		340 Blue Violet-med.
119	◣		333 Blue Violet-dk.
15	╳	◿	775 Baby Blue-lt.
158	·		747 Sky Blue-vy. lt.
167	●		598 Turquoise-lt.
900	◇		928 Slate Green-lt.
378	▲	◣	841 Beige Brown-dk.
380	W	◸	839 Beige Brown
397	✕	◿	453 Shell Gray-lt.
398	▢	◿	415 Pearl Gray

Step 2: Backstitch (one strand)

922	L		930 Antique Blue-dk.

Step 3: Bow

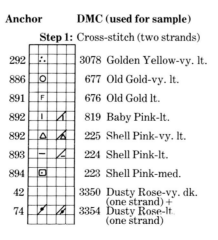

Where ribbon comes in and out (around neck of goose)

FABRICS	DESIGN SIZES
Aida 11	11″ x 11″
Aida 14	8⅝″ x 8⅝″
Aida 18	6¾″ x 6¾″
Hardanger 22	5½″ x 5½″

On this day, you might order flowers, give her a box of candy, send her a card, or just call. But she'll know she's really appreciated if you take the time to make one of these feminine projects designed especially for mothers.

Floral Mat

SAMPLE
Stitched on cream Aida 14, the finished design size is 11¼″ x 13¼″. The fabric was cut 17″ x 20″. Have the mat cut by a professional framer.

MATERIALS
Completed cross-stitch on cream Aida 14
Professionally cut mat (see Step 1)
Double-sided tape
Masking tape
Dressmakers' pen

DIRECTIONS
1. Have a professional framer cut the mat board. The outside dimensions are 14½″ x 16¾″. The window dimensions are 7¼″ x 9¼″.

2. With design centered, trim the Aida to measure 16½″ x 18¾″.

3. Place the Aida wrong side up on a flat surface. Center the mat over the fabric and trace the edge of the window onto the fabric. Then draw a smaller window 2″ inside the first window. Cut along the inside pencil line. Snip the corners between the two pencil lines at a 45° angle.

4. On the wrong side of the mat, run a strip of double-sided tape along the top edge of the window. Fold the fabric over the mat, making sure that the violet cross-stitched border is parallel to the inside edge of the mat.

5. Repeat Step 4 for the bottom edge of the window; then the side edges.

6. Still on the wrong side of the mat, run a strip of double-sided tape along the top outside edge to within 2″ of the corners. Fold the fabric over the edge, pulling it taut. Repeat along the bottom edge; then the sides. Trim the excess fabric from the corners on the back and secure with masking tape. Place the mat in a ready-made frame or have a professional framer complete the framing.

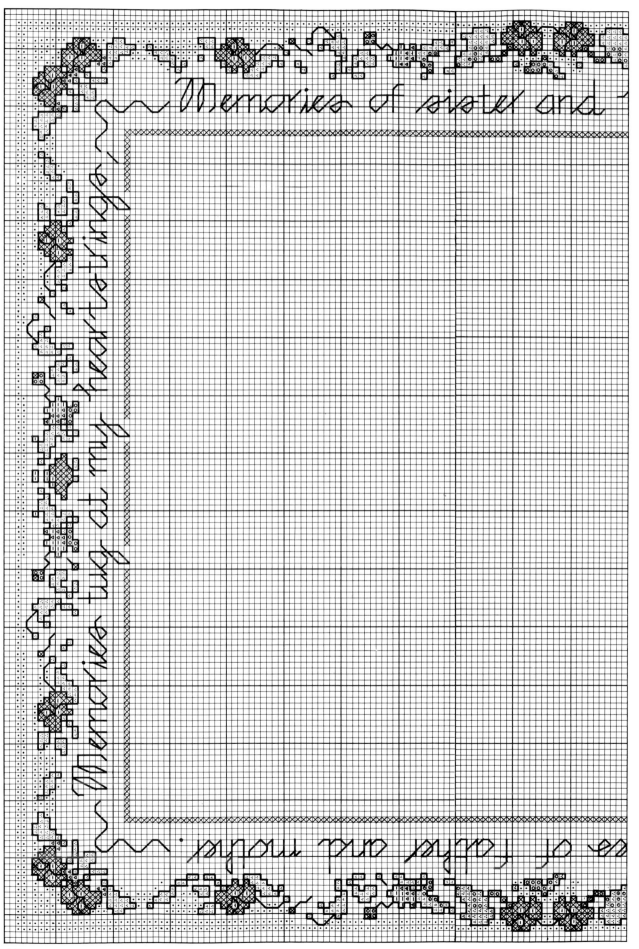

Stitch Count: 158 x 186

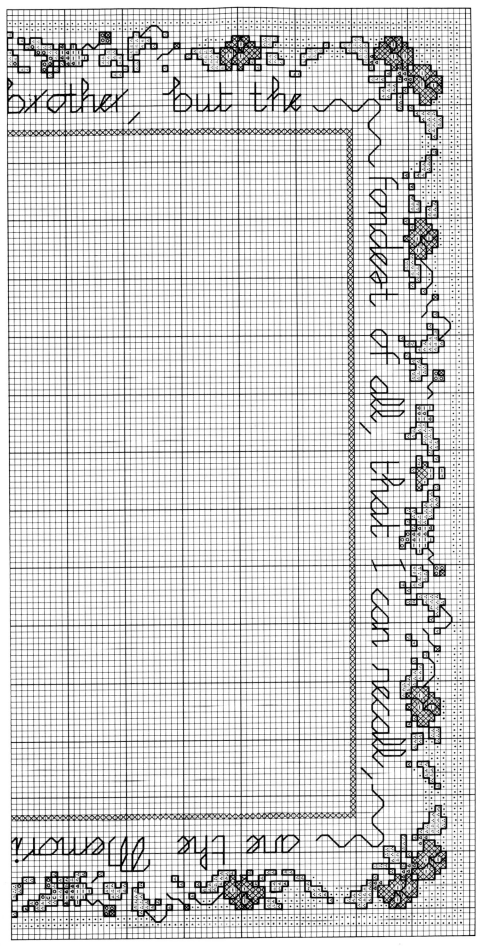

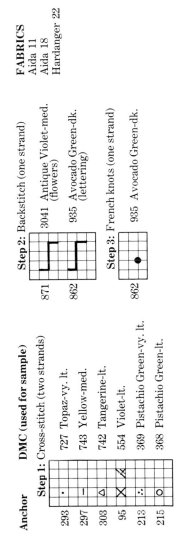

Anchor	DMC (used for sample)							
Step 1: Cross-stitch (two strands)								
293	727	Topaz-vy. lt.						·
297	743	Yellow-med.						—
303	742	Tangerine-lt.						△
95	554	Violet-lt.						✕ / ◩
213	369	Pistachio Green-vy. lt.						∴
215	368	Pistachio Green-lt.						○

Step 2: Backstitch (one strand)

871	3041	Antique Violet-med. (flowers)
862	935	Avocado Green-dk. (lettering)

Step 3: French knots (one strand)

862	935	Avocado Green-dk.

FABRICS
Aida 11
Aida 18
Hardanger 22

DESIGN SIZES
14¼" x 17"
8¾" x 10¼"
7¼" x 8½"

63

Sachet Bags

SAMPLE for Small Bag
Stitched on Glenshee Egyptian Cotton quality D over two threads, the finished design size is 2⅛″ x 2½″. The fabric was cut 8″ x 21″. Center the design 6½″ below the top 8″ edge of the fabric.

MATERIALS
Completed cross-stitch on Glenshee Egyptian Cotton quality D; matching thread
1 yard of ⅛″-wide rose satin ribbon
⅜ yard of ¼″-wide cream flat cotton lace for front
⅜ yard of ⅝″-wide cream flat cotton lace for top
1 cup potpourri

DIRECTIONS for Small Bag

All seam allowances are ¼".

1. Cut the Glenshee Egyptian Cotton 6½" x 19", with design centered horizontally and top of design 5¾" from top 6½" edge.

2. Pin the ⅜"-wide lace ¼" outside design, easing lace at corners and overlapping ends. Slipstitch both edges in place.

3. Fold design piece with right sides together to measure 6½" x 9½". Stitch sides. Do not turn.

4. Fold down top edge of bag 2½" and match side seams. To form casing, turn raw edge under ¼" and stitch around bag close to second fold. Stitch another seam parallel to and ¼" above first row. Turn right side out.

5. Using a seam ripper, carefully cut the threads that are between the two rows of stitching on the outside seams of the bag.

6. Cut ribbon into two equal lengths. Attach a safety pin to end of one piece of ribbon and thread it through opening on one side of bag, past second opening, and back out first opening. Knot ribbon ends. Thread second piece through second opening, past first, and out second. Knot ends.

7. Slipstitch the ⅝"-wide lace to bag just inside top edge, with lace extending up. Fill bag with potpourri. Draw bag closed.

SAMPLE for Large Bag

Stitched on Glenshee Egyptian Cotton quality D over two threads, the finished design size is 2⅛" x 4⅜". The fabric was cut 9" x 23". Center the design 6" below the top 9" edge of the fabric.

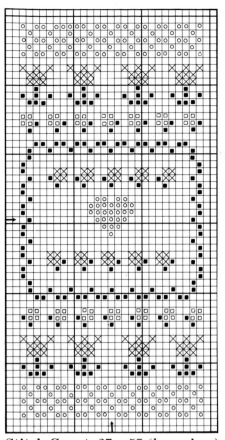

Stitch Count: 27 x 57 (large bag)

MATERIALS

Completed cross-stitch on Glenshee Egyptian Cotton quality
D: matching thread
1½ yards of ⅛"-wide blue satin ribbon
⅝ yard of ½"-wide cream flat cotton lace for front
½ yard of ¾"-wide cream flat cotton lace for top
1½ cups potpourri

DIRECTIONS for Large Bag

1. Cut Glenshee Egyptian Cotton 7" x 21", with design centered horizontally and top of design 4¾" from top 7" edge.

2. Pin the ½"-wide flat lace ¼" outside design, easing lace at corners and overlapping ends. Slipstitch both edges in place.

3. Fold design piece with right sides together to measure 7" x 10½". Stitch sides. Do not turn.

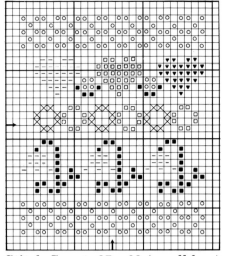

Stitch Count: 27 x 32 (small bag)

4. Complete Steps 4, 5, 6, and 7 of the directions for the small bag, stitching the ¾"-wide lace around the top edge of the bag.

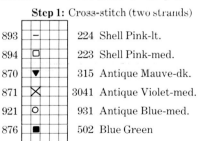

Large Sachet Bag

Anchor		DMC (used for sample)

Step 1: Cross-stitch (two strands)

894	▢	223 Shell Pink-med.
871	✕	3041 Antique Violet-med.
921	O	931 Antique Blue-med.
876	■	502 Blue Green

FABRICS	DESIGN SIZES
Aida 11	2½" x 2⅞"
Aida 14	1⅞" x 2¼"
Aida 18	1½" x 1¾"
Hardanger 22	1¼" x 1½"

Small Sachet Bag

Anchor		DMC (used for sample)

Step 1: Cross-stitch (two strands)

893	–	224 Shell Pink-lt.
894	▢	223 Shell Pink-med.
870	▼	315 Antique Mauve-dk.
871	✕	3041 Antique Violet-med.
921	O	931 Antique Blue-med.
876	■	502 Blue Green

FABRICS	DESIGN SIZES
Aida 11	2½" x 5⅛"
Aida 14	1⅞" x 4⅛"
Aida 18	1½" x 3⅛"
Hardanger 22	1¼" x 2⅝"

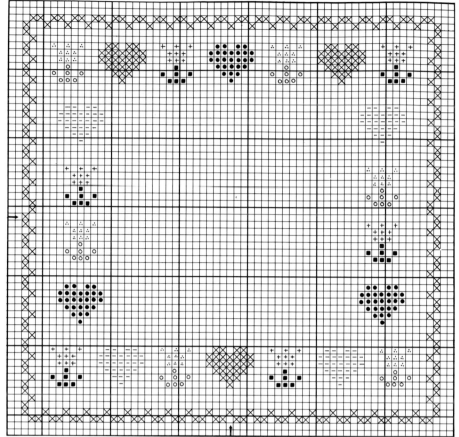

Stitch Count: 61 x 59

Rimini Pillow

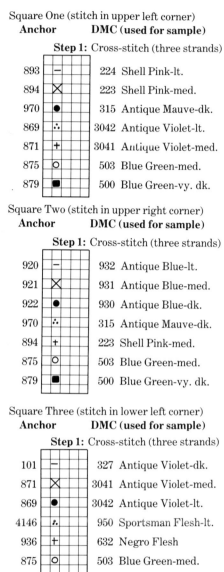

Square One (stitch in upper left corner)

Anchor		DMC (used for sample)
		Step 1: Cross-stitch (three strands)
893	–	224 Shell Pink-lt.
894	X	223 Shell Pink-med.
970	●	315 Antique Mauve-dk.
869	∴	3042 Antique Violet-lt.
871	+	3041 Antique Violet-med.
875	O	503 Blue Green-med.
879	■	500 Blue Green-vy. dk.

Square Two (stitch in upper right corner)

Anchor		DMC (used for sample)
		Step 1: Cross-stitch (three strands)
920	–	932 Antique Blue-lt.
921	X	931 Antique Blue-med.
922	●	930 Antique Blue-dk.
970	∴	315 Antique Mauve-dk.
894	+	223 Shell Pink-med.
875	O	503 Blue Green-med.
879	■	500 Blue Green-vy. dk.

Square Three (stitch in lower left corner)

Anchor		DMC (used for sample)
		Step 1: Cross-stitch (three strands)
101	–	327 Antique Violet-dk.
871	X	3041 Antique Violet-med.
869	●	3042 Antique Violet-lt.
4146	∴	950 Sportsman Flesh-lt.
936	+	632 Negro Flesh
875	O	503 Blue Green-med.
879	■	500 Blue Green-vy. dk.

Square Four (stitch in lower right corner)

Anchor		DMC (used for sample)
		Step 1: Cross-stitch (three strands)
4146	–	950 Sportsman Flesh-lt.
882	X	407 Sportsman Flesh-dk.
936	●	632 Negro Flesh
922	∴	930 Antique Blue-dk.
920	+	932 Antique Blue-lt.
875	O	503 Blue Green-med.
879	■	500 Blue Green-vy. dk.

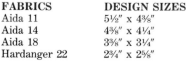

FABRICS	DESIGN SIZES
Aida 11	5½" x 4⅝"
Aida 14	4⅜" x 4¼"
Aida 18	3⅜" x 3¼"
Hardanger 22	2¾" x 2⅝"

SAMPLE

Stitched on cream Rimini 27 over two threads, finished design size for one square is 4½" x 4⅜". Fabric was cut 13" x 13". See Suppliers for information on ordering Rimini.

MATERIALS

Completed cross-stitch on cream Rimini 27; matching thread
One 12¾" x 12¾" piece of rose satin for back
3 yards of 1½"-wide cream flat lace
14" x 14" knife-edge pillow form

DIRECTIONS

All seam allowances are ½".

1. Trim the Rimini 1¼" outside the stitched design.

2. Divide lace into quarters; mark quarters on straight edge. Sew a gathering thread close to straight edge. Gather lace to fit around edge of pillow front.

3. Place straight edge of lace over the outermost woven band on right side of Rimini, with lace toward center of pillow front. Pin lace to pillow front, matching quarter marks to corners and overlapping ends. Sew lace to pillow front.

4. Place pillow front and back, right sides together, keeping lace tucked to inside. Stitch on the stitching line of the lace, leaving a 5" opening. Trim corners. Turn right side out and insert pillow form. Slipstitch opening closed.

MAY 30
Memorial Day

Memorial Day was originally observed in cities and towns across the United States with parades, speeches, and floral tributes to those who had given their lives for their country. Over the years the tradition broadened to become a memorial for all loved ones.

Man's life is laid in the loom of time
To a pattern he does not see,
While weavers work and shuttles fly
Till the dawn of eternity.

Loom of Time

SAMPLE
Stitched on cream Linda 27 over two threads, the finished design size is 8⅞" x 7⅝". Fabric was cut 15" x 14".

Anchor		DMC (used for sample)
Step 1: Cross-stitch (two strands)		
926	U	Ecru
292	K	3078 Golden Yellow-vy. lt.
778	•	948 Peach Flesh-vy. lt.
868	–	758 Terra Cotta-lt.
892	A	225 Shell Pink-vy. lt.
24	J	776 Pink-med.
41	I	335 Rose
42	+	309 Rose-deep
970	⧄	315 Antique Mauve-dk.
44	∴	816 Garnet
95	O	554 Violet-lt.
98	■	553 Violet-med.
105	▽	209 Lavender-dk.
110	●	208 Lavender-vy. dk.
101	O	327 Antique Violet-dk.

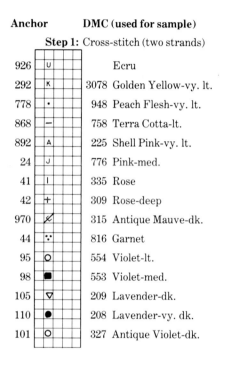

159	∴	827 Blue-vy. lt.
213	•	369 Pistachio Green-vy. lt.
214	▢	966 Baby Green-med.
209	▲	913 Nile Green-med.
208	X	563 Jade-lt.
210	X	562 Jade-med.
187		992 Aquamarine
189	▢	991 Aquamarine-dk.
879	N	500 Blue Green-vy. dk.
914	△	3064 Sportsman Flesh-med.
936	⊥	632 Negro Flesh
378	S	841 Beige Brown-lt.
380	H	839 Beige Brown-dk.
381	E	838 Beige Brown-vy. dk.
399	Z	451 Shell Gray-dk.
401	B	413 Pewter Gray-dk.

Step 2: Backstitch (one strand)

101		327 Antique Violet-dk. (lettering)
381		838 Beige Brown-vy. dk. (all else)

Step 3: French knots (one strand)

101	●	327 Antique Violet-dk.

FABRICS	DESIGN SIZES
Aida 11	10⅞" x 9⅜"
Aida 14	8⅝" x 7⅜"
Aida 18	6⅝" x 5¾"
Hardanger 22	5½" x 4⅝"

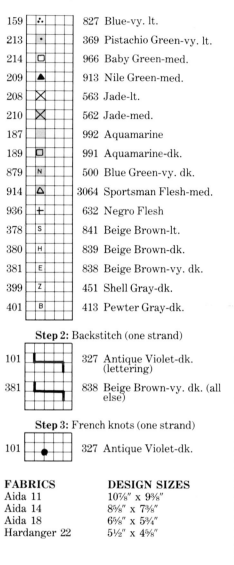

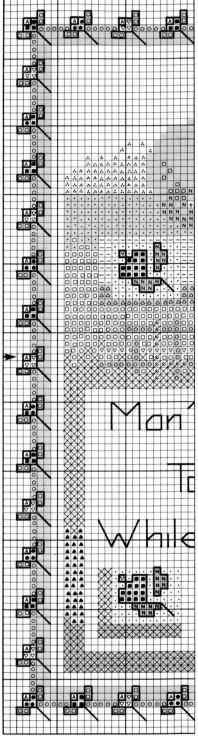

Stitch Count: 120 x 103

s life is laid in the loom of time

o a pattern he does not see,

weavers work and shuttles fly

Till the dawn of eternity.

Father's Day

Since 1910, this day has been set aside to pay tribute to fathers. Today, fathers do much more than just "bring home the bacon." They provide strong and caring masculine role models. Now, more than ever, fathers are realizing the joys of creating close bonds with their children. As one dad says, "We've come a long way, baby and me."

Coverlet

SAMPLE

The throw was stitched on toasted rye Ragusa 14. The fabric was cut 56″ x 72″. Begin stitching corner design 4½″ from the right corner of one short edge. (The heavy black lines on the graph indicate where the border begins.) Then stitch the border (see Father's Day Sampler) on one long edge, working in the following sequence: Repeat #1, #2, #1, #2, #1 and the corner design. Continuing to stitch counterclockwise, work short edge in the following sequence from the corner design: Repeat #1, #2, #1, #2 and the corner design. Stitch remaining long edge and short edge.

MATERIALS

Completed cross-stitch on toasted rye Ragusa 14

DIRECTIONS

1. Trim Ragusa 4″ outside the stitched design all around. Fringe 3″ of fabric on all edges.

2. Handling four threads of fringe as a single unit, tie a knot close to the edge of the fabric. Repeat with the fringe all around the coverlet.

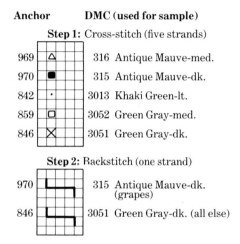

Anchor		DMC (used for sample)	
		Step 1: Cross-stitch (five strands)	
969	△	316	Antique Mauve-med.
970	■	315	Antique Mauve-dk.
842	·	3013	Khaki Green-lt.
859	□	3052	Green Gray-med.
846	✕	3051	Green Gray-dk.
		Step 2: Backstitch (one strand)	
970		315	Antique Mauve-dk. (grapes)
846		3051	Green Gray-dk. (all else)

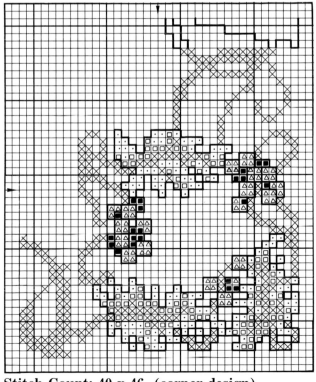

Stitch Count: 40 x 46 (corner design)

The poor man
is not he who is
without a cent,
but he who is
without a dream.

SNB 1990

Stitch Count: 130 x 110

Repeat #1

Repeat #2

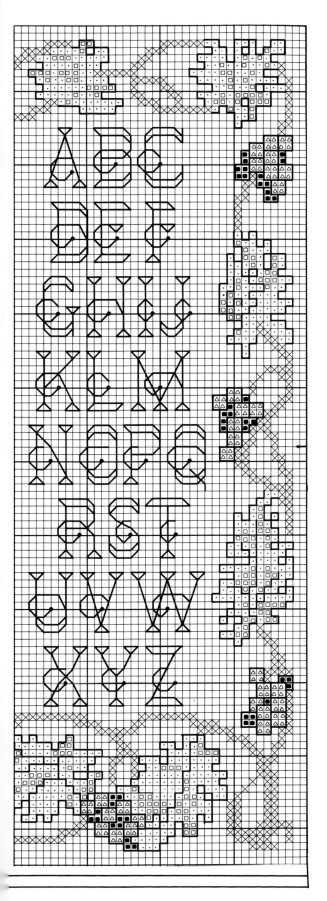

Father's Day Sampler

SAMPLE

Stitched on cream Aida 14, the finished design size is 9¼" x 7⅞". The fabric was cut 16" x 14". To add your initials and the date, transfer letters and numbers to graph paper. Mark the center of the graph and begin stitching in the center of the space indicated for personalizing.

Anchor		DMC (used for sample)

Step 1: Cross-stitch (two strands)

969	△	316 Antique Mauve-med.
970	■	315 Antique Mauve-dk.
842	·	3013 Khaki Green-lt.
859	□	3052 Green Gray-med.
846	✕	3051 Green Gray-dk.

Step 2: Backstitch (one strand)

969		316 Antique Mauve-med. (alphabet, initials, date)
970		315 Antique Mauve-dk. (saying)
846		3051 Green Gray-dk. (all else)

Step 3: French knots (one strand)

969	●	316 Antique Mauve-med.
970	◆	315 Antique Mauve-dk.
846	○	3051 Green Gray-dk.

FABRICS	DESIGN SIZES
Aida 11	11⅞" x 10"
Aida 18	7¼" x 6⅛"
Hardanger 22	5⅞" x 5"

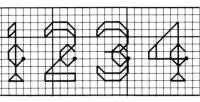

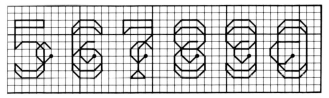

JULY
Peach Days

Refresh yourself on those hot July days with a bite into a sweet juicy peach! This delectable treat, native to China, was first cultivated at least 3,000 years ago. The fruit was brought to America during the 16th century by Spanish settlers. Today peaches are a favorite summer treat, but they can be enjoyed year-round in pies, preserves, or even right from the can. Here are two more peachy ideas to brighten up your kitchen!

Ripe peaches
on a 🍑
summer's eve,
the stone's
the only part
you leave.

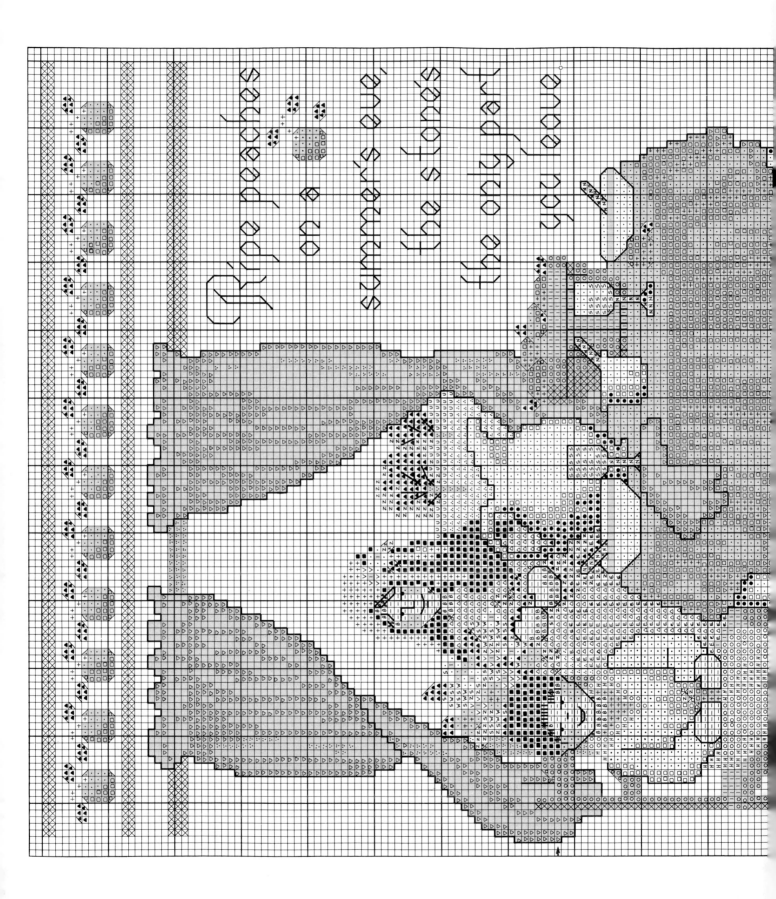

Stitch Count: 116 x 155

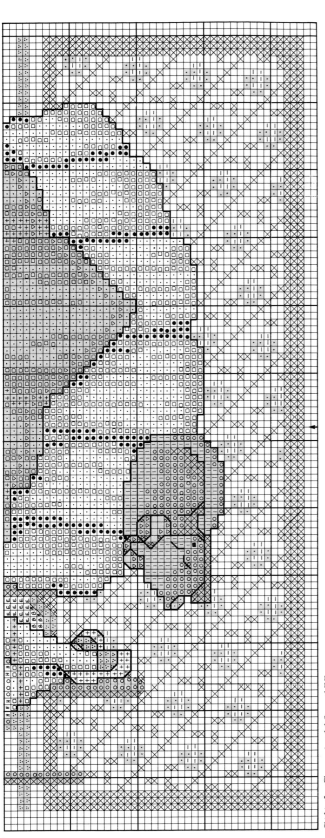

Just Peachy

SAMPLES

Hand Towel: The design, taken from the top of the sampler graph, was stitched on a white-and-blue waffle towel. Begin stitching near the left edge of the Aida area, leaving three threads empty above the design and two below the design. Continue the pattern to the right edge of the Aida area.

Sampler: Stitched on white Hardanger 22 over two threads, the finished design size is 10½" x 14⅛". The fabric was cut 17" x 21".

Anchor		DMC (used for sample)
		Step 1: Cross-stitch (three strands)
1		White
386		746 Off White
4146		754 Peach Flesh-lt.
868		758 Terra Cotta-lt.
8		353 Peach Flesh
10		352 Coral-lt.
11		3328 Salmon-med.
85		3609 Plum-ultra lt.
86		3608 Plum-vy. lt.
98		553 Violet-med.
101		550 Violet-vy. dk.
158		775 Baby Blue-lt.
128		800 Delft-pale
131		798 Delft-dk.
941		791 Cornflower Blue-vy. dk.

Anchor		DMC
213		504 Blue Green-lt.
875		503 Blue Green-med.
214		368 Pistachio Green-lt.
215		320 Pistachio Green-med.
246		319 Pistachio Green-vy. dk.
362		437 Tan-lt.
309		435 Brown-vy. lt.
371		433 Brown-med.
378		841 Beige Brown-lt.
379		840 Beige Brown-med.
381		838 Beige Brown-vy. dk.
397		762 Pearl Gray-vy. lt.
398		415 Pearl Gray
400		414 Steel Gray-dk.

Step 2: Backstitch (one strand)

11	3328 Salmon-med. (tablecloth)

Anchor	DMC
13	347 Salmon-dk. (mouths)
131	798 Delft-dk. (curtains, cat's ribbon, napkin)
246	319 Pistachio Green-vy. dk. (lettering)
371	433 Brown-med. (basket)
379	840 Beige Brown-med. (hands, around face)
381	838 Beige Brown-vy. dk. (hair, noses, eyes, tree branches, shoes, cat)
400	414 Steel Gray-dk. (all else)

Step 3: French knots (one strand)

941	791 Cornflower Blue-vy. dk.
246	319 Pistachio Green-vy. dk.

DESIGN SIZES

FABRICS	DESIGN SIZES
Aida 11	10½" x 14⅛"
Aida 14	8¾" x 11⅛"
Aida 18	6½" x 8⅝"
Hardanger 22	5¼" x 7"

JULY 4
Independence Day

Fireworks, parades, and red-white-and-blue! Americans salute the birth of their nation with spectacular celebrations. The day is filled with fun: picnics, flag-raisings, and baseball games. It ends with an explosion of brilliant color and flashing lights. Add a dash of Americana to your home with one or all of these striking patriotic pillows!

Pillow Trio

SAMPLES

Liberty Flag Pillow:
Stitched on light brown Linen 26 over two threads, the finished design size is 9½" x 7". The fabric was cut 15" x 13".

Stars & Stripes and Confederate Pillow:
Stitched on light brown Linen 26 over two threads, the finished design size is 9⅝" x 7¼". The fabric was cut 15" x 13".

MATERIALS (for one pillow)
Completed cross-stitch on light brown Linen 26
1 yard of 45"-wide bronze satin fabric; matching thread
1½ yards of medium cording
Stuffing

DIRECTIONS
All seam allowances are ¼".

1. Trim linen to 11" x 8½" with design centered.

2. From satin fabric, cut one 15½" x 12½" piece for the back of the pillow. Also cut two 16" x 3" pieces and two 13" x 3" pieces for the border. Cut a 1¼"-wide bias strip, piecing as needed to equal 1½ yards.

3. To make 1½ yards of corded piping, place the cording in the center of the wrong side of the bias strip and fold the fabric over it. Using a zipper foot, stitch close to the cording through both layers of fabric. Trim the seam allowance ¼" from the stitching line.

4. Mark the center of one long edge of each border strip and the center of each edge of the design piece. With right sides together and center marks matching, sew the border strips to the front of the design piece. Stitch to within ¼" of each corner; backstitch. Press seams toward border.

5. To miter the corners, fold the right sides of two adjacent strips together and sew at a 45-degree angle (see Diagram). Trim the seam allowance to ¼". Repeat for remaining corners.

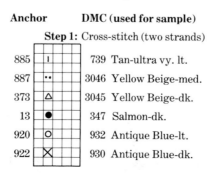

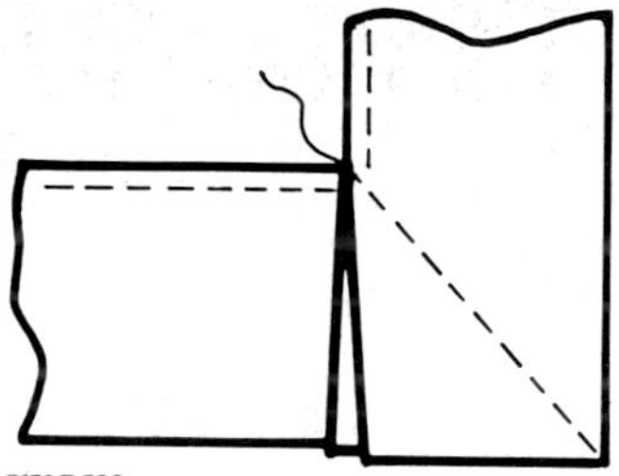

Diagram

6. With raw edges aligned, stitch the piping to the right side of the pillow front. Then, with right sides together, stitch the pillow front to the back, sewing on the stitching line of the piping. Leave an opening for turning. Clip the corners and turn right side out. Stuff. Slipstitch the opening closed.

Stars & Stripes Pillow

Anchor		DMC (used for sample)

Step 1: Cross-stitch (two strands)

885	I	739 Tan-ultra vy. lt.
887	••	3046 Yellow Beige-med.
373	△	3045 Yellow Beige-dk.
13	●	347 Salmon-dk.
920	○	932 Antique Blue-lt.
922	✕	930 Antique Blue-dk.

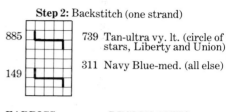

Step 2: Backstitch (one strand)

| 885 | | 739 Tan-ultra vy. lt. (circle of stars, Liberty and Union) |
| 149 | | 311 Navy Blue-med. (all else) |

FABRICS	DESIGN SIZES
Aida 11	11" x 8⅛"
Aida 14	8⅝" x 6⅜"
Aida 18	6¾" x 5"
Hardanger 22	5½" x 4"

Liberty Flag Pillow

Anchor		DMC (used for sample)

Step 1: Cross-stitch (two strands)

885	I ╱	739 Tan-ultra vy. lt.
887	••	3046 Yellow Beige-med.
373	△	3045 Yellow Beige-dk.
13	●	347 Salmon-dk.
922	✕ ╱	930 Antique Blue-dk.
861	■ ╱	3363 Pine Green-med.

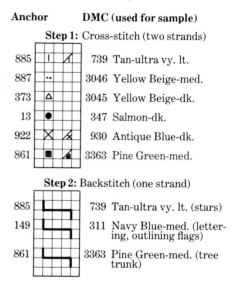

Step 2: Backstitch (one strand)

885		739 Tan-ultra vy. lt. (stars)
149		311 Navy Blue-med. (lettering, outlining flags)
861		3363 Pine Green-med. (tree trunk)

Confederate Pillow

Anchor		DMC (used for sample)

Step 1: Cross-stitch (two strands)

885	I	739 Tan-ultra vy. lt.
887	••	3046 Yellow Beige-med.
373	△	3045 Yellow Beige-dk.
13	●	347 Salmon-dk.
922	✕	930 Antique Blue-dk.
889	□	610 Drab Brown-vy. dk.

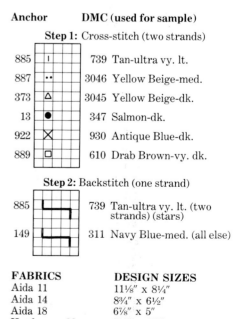

Step 2: Backstitch (one strand)

| 885 | | 739 Tan-ultra vy. lt. (two strands) (stars) |
| 149 | | 311 Navy Blue-med. (all else) |

FABRICS	DESIGN SIZES
Aida 11	11⅛" x 8¼"
Aida 14	8¾" x 6½"
Aida 18	6⅞" x 5"
Hardanger 22	5⅝" x 4⅛"

Stitch Count: 123 x 91

81

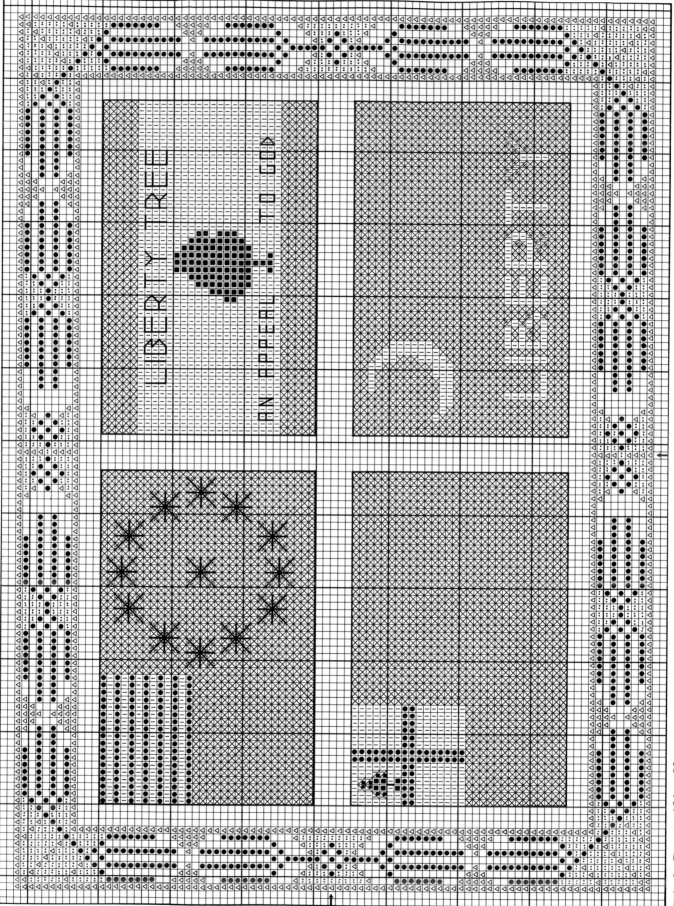

LIBERTY TREE

AN APPEAL TO GOD

Stitch Count: 121 x 89

Stitch Count: 123 x 91

Vermont Quilt Festival

Women, patches, and lots of needles and thread—all could be found at an old-fashioned quilting bee. Although quilts originally were made to keep people warm on cold winter nights, now they serve as an outlet of artistic expression. Today, quilt lovers flock to Northfield, Vermont, to participate in classes, to exhibit their own creations, or just to enjoy the wide variety of quilts displayed, as the Vermont Quilt Festival applauds the American art of quiltmaking.

Northern Neighbors

SAMPLE
Stitched on natural Super Linen 27 over two threads, the finished design size is 5¼" x 6¾". The fabric was cut 11" x 13".

Stitch Count: 70 x 90

Anchor			DMC (used for sample)
			Step 1: Cross-stitch (two strands)
868	··	◿	758 Terra Cotta-lt.
9	+	◿	760 Salmon
11	▼	◿	3328 Salmon-med.
158	△		775 Baby Blue-lt.
145	✕		334 Baby Blue-med.

167	◿		598 Turquoise-lt.
187	■		992 Aquamarine
213	○		504 Blue Green-lt.
875	▢		503 Blue Green-med.
878	●	◿	501 Blue Green-dk.
885	❙	◿	739 Tan-ultra vy. lt.
362	=		437 Tan-lt.

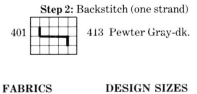

Step 2: Backstitch (one strand)

401	⌐	413 Pewter Gray-dk.

FABRICS
Aida 11
Aida 14
Aida 18
Hardanger 22

DESIGN SIZES
6⅜" x 8⅛"
5" x 6⅜"
3⅞" x 5"
3⅛"x 4⅛"

85

AUGUST 11
Night of the Shooting Stars

"Starlight, star bright, first star I see tonight, I wish I may, I wish I might, have the wish I wish tonight!" Children all over the world will be filled with wonder as they watch stars falling on this magical night.

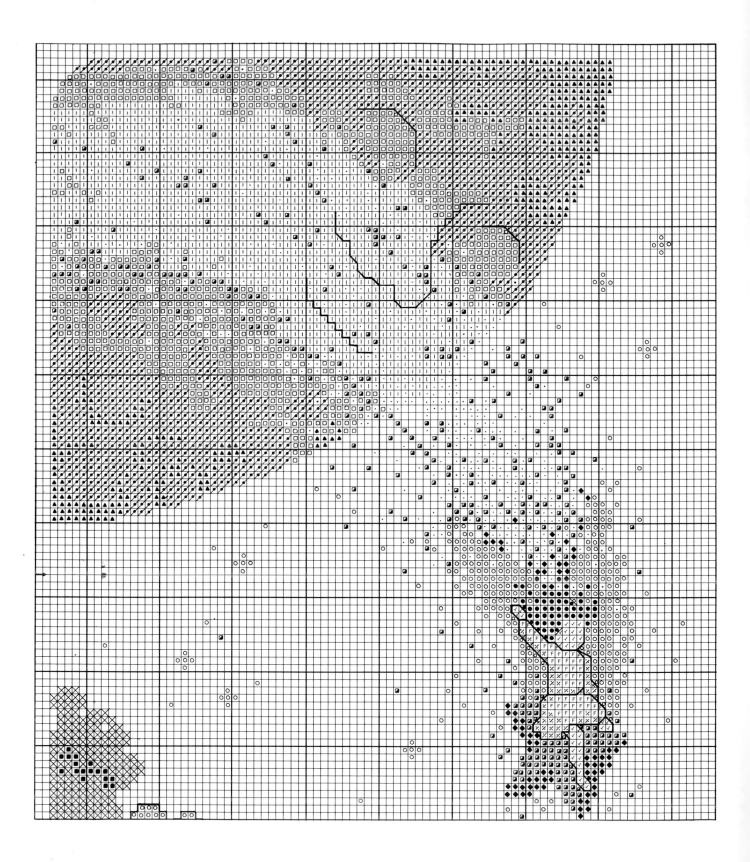

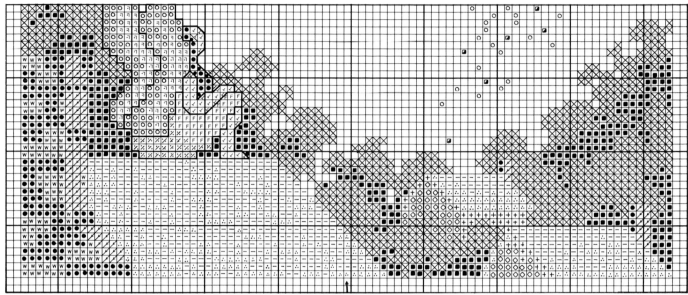

Stitch Count: 89 x 140

Starlight, Star Bright

SAMPLE

Stitched on navy Lugana 25 over two threads, the finished design size is 7⅛″ x 11¼″. The Lugana was cut 14″ x 18″.

Anchor			DMC (used for sample)
			Step 1: Cross-stitch (two strands)
926	•		Ecru (1 strand) +
			032 Pearl Balger (2 strands)
926	O	◢	Ecru
881	⟋	◸	948 Peach Flesh-vy. lt.
301	◪	◸	744 Yellow-pale
297	◆	◂	743 Yellow-med.
886	I		677 Old Gold-vy. lt.
891	◻	◸	676 Old Gold-lt.
890	⟋	◸	729 Old Gold-med.
901	▲		680 Old Gold-dk.
108	F	◸	211 Lavender-lt.
104	╱	◸	210 Lavender-med.
128	⅂	◸	800 Delft-pale
215	X	◸	320 Pistachio Green-med.
246	■	◸	319 Pistachio Green-vy. dk.
5975	–		356 Terra Cotta-med.
5968	∴		355 Terra Cotta-dk.
349	⟋		301 Mahogany-med.
351	●	◸	400 Mahogany-dk.
376	◇		842 Beige Brown-vy. lt.
378	+		841 Beige Brown-lt.
357	w		801 Coffee Brown-dk.

			Step 2: Backstitch (one strand)
127	⌐	939	Navy Blue-vy. dk. (around angels)
357	⌐	801	Coffee Brown-dk. (all else)

FABRICS	DESIGN SIZES
Aida 11	8⅛″ x 12¾″
Aida 14	6⅜″ x 10″
Aida 18	5″ x 7¾″
Hardanger 22	4″ x 6⅜″

SEPTEMBER 9
Grandparents' Day

Where can one find a wealth of knowledge, understanding, and hundreds of stories about how life used to be? Why, of course, from all of those loving grandparents just waiting to share their experiences. Grandparents' Day has been set aside to honor these very special people in our lives.

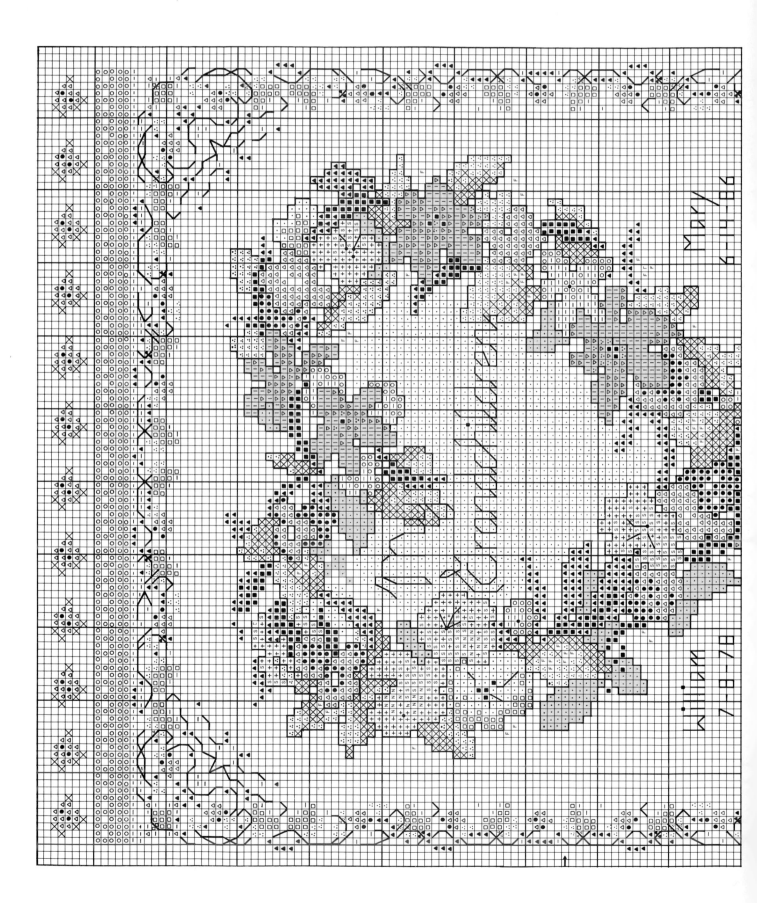

Stitch Count: 109 x 143

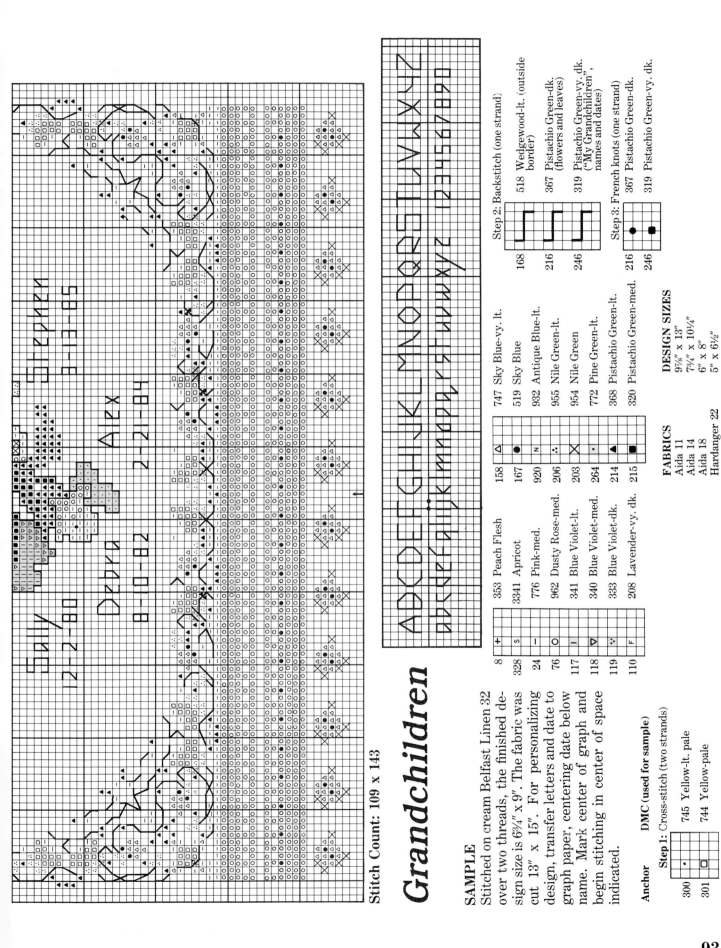

Grandchildren

SAMPLE

Stitched on cream Belfast Linen 32 over two threads, the finished design size is 6¾" x 9". The fabric was cut 13" x 15". For personalizing design, transfer letters and date to graph paper, centering date below name. Mark center of graph and begin stitching in center of space indicated.

Anchor	DMC (used for sample)

Step 1: Cross-stitch (two strands)

300	•	745 Yellow-lt. pale
301	□	744 Yellow-pale

8	+	353 Peach Flesh
328	s	3341 Apricot
24	▬	776 Pink-med.
76	O	962 Dusty Rose-med.
117	I	341 Blue Violet-lt.
118	▷	340 Blue Violet-med.
119	∴	333 Blue Violet-dk.
110	F	208 Lavender-vy. dk.

158	◁	747 Sky Blue-vy. lt.
167	●	519 Sky Blue
920	N	932 Antique Blue-lt.
206	∴	955 Nile Green-lt.
203	✕	954 Nile Green
264	•	772 Pine Green-lt.
214	◀	368 Pistachio Green-lt.
215	■	320 Pistachio Green-med.

Step 2: Backstitch (one strand)

168		518 Wedgewood-lt. (outside border)
216		367 Pistachio Green-dk. (flowers and leaves)
246		319 Pistachio Green-vy. dk. ("My Grandchildren", names and dates)

Step 3: French knots (one strand)

216	●	367 Pistachio Green-dk.
246	■	319 Pistachio Green-vy. dk.

FABRICS

FABRICS	DESIGN SIZES
Aida 11	9⅞" x 13"
Aida 14	7¾" x 10¼"
Aida 18	6" x 8"
Hardanger 22	5" x 6½"

93

SEPTEMBER 12
National Hunting & Fishing Day

Sportsmen who enjoy the outdoors and thrill at the thought of landing a prize bass or bringing home a big buck are also aware of the need to ensure that these opportunities will always be there for others. For their contribution to the conservation and protection of our natural resources, sportsmen are honored on this day.

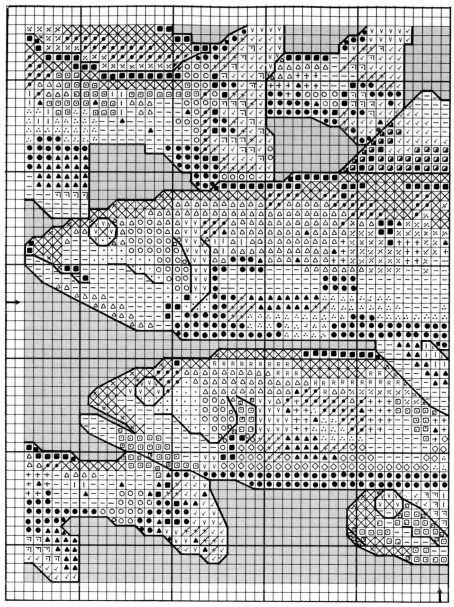

Stitch Count: 90 x 60

Rainbow Trout

SAMPLE

Stitched on cream Aida 14, the finished design size is 6⅜″ x 4¼″. The fabric was cut 13″ x 11″. Floss and Balger blending filament are combined, sometimes in two strands and sometimes in three, to stitch this design. Become familiar with the information in the code before you begin stitching the design.

* Mix with one strand of Star Yellow Balger (091) high luster.

~ Mix with one strand of C Copper Balger (021) cord.

Mix with one strand of Peacock Balger (085) blending filament.

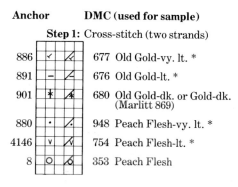

Anchor			DMC (used for sample)
			Step 1: Cross-stitch (two strands)
886	✓	◿	677 Old Gold-vy. lt. *
891	–	◿	676 Old Gold-lt. *
901	�	◢	680 Old Gold-dk. or Gold-dk. (Marlitt 869)
880	·	◿	948 Peach Flesh-vy. lt. *
4146	v	◿	754 Peach Flesh-lt. *
8	O	◿	353 Peach Flesh

			DMC / Color
11	▲	◢	3328 Salmon-med. (2 strands) ~
11	⌐		3328 Salmon-med. (2 strands) #
158	+		747 Sky Blue-vy. lt. *
160	۱	╱	813 Blue-lt. *
779	(shaded)	╱	926 Slate Green-dk.
266	╱	◢	3347 Yellow Green-med. *
266	△	◢	3347 Yellow Green-med. (1 strand) +
859			522 Fern Green (1 strand) *
227	◢	◢	701 Christmas Green-lt. (1 strand) + / 216 367 Pistachio Green-dk. (1 strand) *
859 216	⊡	◢	522 Fern Green (1 strand) + / 367 Pistachio Green-dk. (1 strand) *

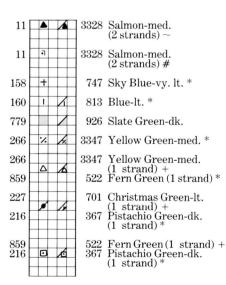

859 216	◪	◢	522 Fern Green (1 strand) + / 367 Pistachio Green-dk. (1 strand) #
216	R	◀	367 Pistachio Green-dk. *
216			367 Pistachio Green-dk. (1 strand) +
879	✕	◿	500 Blue Green-vy. dk. (1 strand) #
879	■		500 Blue Green-vy. dk. #
347	◇		402 Mahogany-vy. lt. *
347	●		402 Mahogany-vy. lt. ~
347			402 Mahogany-vy. lt. (1 strand) +
4146	∴		754 Peach Flesh-lt. (1 strand) ~

Step 2: Backstitch (one strand)

879 ⌐ 500 Blue Green-vy. dk.

FABRICS
Aida 11
Aida 18
Hardanger 22

DESIGN SIZES
8⅛" x 5½"
5" x 3⅜"
4⅛" x 2¾"

OCTOBER 9
Alphabet Day

One of the first things children learn to recite is the alphabet. Soon, they can decipher the funny scratches that are known as letters. They form the letters into their names and then, gradually, into hundreds and thousands of words. Alphabet Day originated in Korea when, on this day in 1446, the king issued a proclamation giving his people a new alphabet. Having their own national alphabet was a source of great pride to Koreans. Nowadays, to celebrate, they hold calligraphy contests for young and old. Stitch this alphabet sampler as is, or choose your favorite letter and create one of these special keepsakes.

Alphabet Sampler

SAMPLE

Stitched on white Quaker Cloth 28 over two threads, the finished design size is 13⅝" x 17⅞". The fabric was cut 18" x 22".

Anchor			DMC (used for sample)	
	Step 1: Cross-stitch (two strands)			
300	–	⁄	745	Yellow-lt. pale
4146	⊡	◿	754	Peach Flesh-lt.
8	N		353	Peach Flesh
49	�	◿	3689	Mauve-lt.
66	+	◿	3688	Mauve-med.
108	△	◿	211	Lavender-lt.
95	ꞁ		554	Violet-lt.

Anchor			DMC	
128	U	⁄	800	Delft-pale
117	▲		341	Blue Violet-lt.
118	∴	◿	340	Blue Violet-med.
206	O		955	Nile Green-lt.
208	✕		563	Jade-lt.
210	●	◣	562	Jade-med.
882	■	◣	407	Sportsman Flesh-dk.
379	S	◿	840	Beige Brown-med.

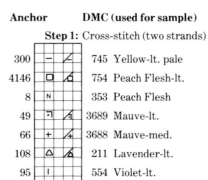

100

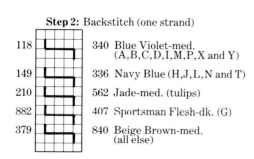

Step 2: Backstitch (one strand)

118		340 Blue Violet-med. (A,B,C,D,I,M,P,X and Y)
149		336 Navy Blue (H,J,L,N and T)
210		562 Jade-med. (tulips)
882		407 Sportsman Flesh-dk. (G)
379		840 Beige Brown-med. (all else)

Step 3: French knots

117		341 Blue Violet-lt.
149		336 Navy Blue
379		840 Beige Brown-med.

FABRICS
Aida 11
Aida 14
Aida 18
Hardanger 22

DESIGN SIZES
17¼″ x 22¾″
13⅝″ x 17⅞″
10⅝″ x 13⅞″
8⅝″ x 11⅜″

Stitch Count: 190 x 251

102

103

Framed Piece

SAMPLE
The letter G was stitched on white Quaker Cloth 28 over two threads. Finished design size is 2¾" x 3½". Fabric was cut 6" x 6".

MATERIALS
Completed cross-stitch on white Quaker Cloth 28; heavy-duty matching thread
13" square of unstitched white Quaker Cloth 28
3½" x 4" piece of foam core
⅓ yard of 1"-wide white satin bias tape
One small tube of green watercolor paint
½"-wide paintbrush
9" x 9" picture frame
Tracing paper

DIRECTIONS
All seam allowances are ¼".

1. Using tracing paper, trace outline of completed design piece and cut out to make a pattern. Trace the pattern onto the piece of foam core and cut out.

2. Trim the design piece ¼" outside the edge of the stitching. Fold under the ends of the bias tape and press. With right sides together and raw edges aligned, stitch the long edge of the bias tape to the edge of design piece, overlapping folded ends. Clip curves.

3. With right side up, place the design piece on the foam core shape, folding bias tape to back. To secure the design piece around the foam core shape, use two strands of thread and stitch through the free edge of the bias tape. Lace stitches diagonally across the foam core, from one side of the shape to the other and then from top to bottom. Set aside.

4. To paint the unstitched square of Quaker cloth, prepare a wash with green watercolor. (Wash should be thin enough for color to spread.) Test color by brushing a small amount on a scrap; allow to dry. When desired consistency is attained, lay the 13" square of Quaker cloth on a flat, protected surface and paint. Let dry.

5. Frame the watercolored fabric. Glue design piece on foam core in lower left corner of frame, 1" from the bottom and left edges.

Crochet Pillow

SAMPLE
The letter L was stitched on white Quaker Cloth 28 over two threads. Finished design size is 2¼" x 3¾". Fabric was cut 7¾" x 9".

MATERIALS
Completed cross-stitch on white Quaker Cloth 28; matching thread
⅛ yard unstitched white Quaker Cloth 28, or matching white fabric for back
1 skein Berroco Dante nubbly yarn, color 1086
Size F crochet hook
Stuffing
36 teardrop glass beads

DIRECTIONS
All seam allowances are ¼".

1. Trim the Quaker cloth to 3¾" x 5" with design centered. Cut one 3¾" x 5" piece for the back and one 16" x 2" strip for the boxing.

2. With right sides together and raw edges aligned, stitch the ends of the boxing strip together. Then stitch one long edge of the boxing piece to the design piece, right sides together.

3. With right sides together, stitch the boxing to the pillow back, leaving a 3" opening for turning. Turn right side out and stuff. Slipstitch the opening closed.

4. Crochet the trim. Make a chain 15" long; join with a slipstitch in beginning chain. For Round 1, insert hook in next chain, wrap yarn around a left-hand finger to make a 1" loop. Holding loop on finger, complete single-crochet loopstitch as usual. Remove finger from loop. Repeat single-crochet loopstitch around chain. Repeat Round 1, working loopstitch in each stitch around until trim measures 1¼" wide.

5. Slipstitch trim around pillow at top seam. Stitch beads to loops, spacing evenly around pillow.

Covered Box

SAMPLE
The letter N was stitched on white Quaker Cloth 28 over two threads. Finished design size is 3¼" x 2¼". Fabric was cut 7" x 5".

MATERIALS
Completed cross-stitch on white Quaker Cloth 28
½ yard of 45"-wide lavender/blue striped fabric
½ yard of 45"-wide lavender fabric
½ yard ½"-wide flat eyelet trim
⅔ yard ⅝"-wide lavender/pink variegated silk ribbon
1⅓ yards thin cording
22" x 28" piece of posterboard
5½" x 3" piece of corrugated cardboard
⅛ yard of polyester fleece
¼"-wide shank button
½"-wide green glass heart

DIRECTIONS
All seam allowances are ¼".

1. With design centered, trim the Quaker cloth to 4¼" x 3¼". Cut a 4¼" x 3¼" piece of fleece. Baste the fleece to the wrong side of design piece. On the right side of the design piece, with the decorative edge of the eyelet toward the center, align the straight edge of the eyelet with the raw edge of the design piece. Stitch, easing in fullness at the corners and securing the fleece in the seam. Trim the fleece and press seam allowance toward design. Set aside.

2. For box, from striped fabric, cut one 6" x 45" piece for sides and four 7" x 4¾" pieces (for lid, lid lining, and bottom). From lavender fabric, cut 2¼"-wide bias strips, piecing as needed, to equal 44". To make 44" of corded piping, place the cording in the center of the wrong side of the bias strip and fold the fabric over it. Using a zipper foot, stitch close to the cording through both layers of fabric. Cut into two 22" pieces. Set aside.

3. From posterboard, cut two 6¼" x 4" pieces (for bottom and lid of box) and one 21¼" x 2¾" piece for sides. From fleece, cut two 6¼" x 4" pieces.

4. To make the top of box lid, on the right side of one 7" x 4¾" piece of striped fabric, mark ½" from one 4¾" (right) edge and ¾" from the adjacent 7" (bottom) edge. Place design piece on marks. To attach the design piece to the striped fabric, stitch in-the-ditch around the design piece. Pin one length of the piping around the edge of the striped fabric, right sides together, with the raw edge of the piping extending beyond the edge of the striped fabric. Align stitching line of piping with seam line of the striped fabric and stitch along piping stitching line, clipping to the stitching line at corners.

5. Lay one piece of fleece on one of the 6¼" x 4" pieces of posterboard. Lay top of box lid on the fleece, folding piping seam allowance to back of posterboard. Glue seam allowance to posterboard, overlapping it at corners.

6. Center the corrugated cardboard piece on the wrong side of another 7" x 4¾" piece of striped fabric. Glue the raw edges of the fabric to the back of the cardboard. Then center the wrong side of the covered cardboard on the back of the box lid, covering raw edges of piping seam allowance; glue. Stitch buttons to the front of the lid; see photo for placement.

7. To make the box bottom, center a posterboard rectangle on the wrong side of a third 7" x 4¾" piece of striped fabric. Glue raw edges of fabric to the back of posterboard. Glue remaining piece of corded piping around the wrong side of the covered box bottom, aligning the finished edge of the piping with edge of box bottom.

8. Measure and score all marked lines on the 21¼" piece of posterboard (see Diagram). Fold on scored lines to form a box. Fold the 6" x 45" piece of striped fabric, with right sides together, to measure 3" wide. Stitch long edge to form a casing. Turn. Insert scored posterboard into casing, shirring fabric evenly onto posterboard piece. Push fabric back to expose ends of posterboard piece; overlap ¾" and glue ends together. Adjust fabric; slipstitch ends together. Glue the bottom edges of the finished box sides to box bottom.

3½"	4"	6¼"	4"	3½"

Diagram

9. To finish the inside of the box, trim the remaining posterboard rectangle to fit snugly inside the bottom. Trim the remaining piece of fleece to fit the posterboard. Remove from box and stack posterboard, fleece, and the fourth 7" x 4¾" piece of striped fabric. Fold the raw edges of fabric to the back of the posterboard and glue. Glue the wrong side of the covered piece into bottom of box.

10. Tack the shirred fabric at the corners to hold in place. Place the lid on box. Wrap the ribbon around the box and tie a bow on top.

OCTOBER 31
Halloween

Even the least superstitious folks are wary on Halloween. Creepy spiders, ghastly ghouls, and glowing pumpkins may make even the bravest among us just a little bit apprehensive. But have no fear if this black cat crosses your path—it's only a spirited trick-or-treater up to some merry mischief!

Cat Sweatshirt

SAMPLE
Stitched on Waste Canvas 14, the finished design size is 8⅞" x 6⅜". The canvas was cut 12" x 10".

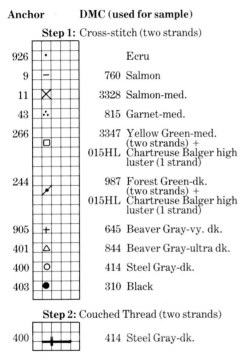

Anchor		DMC (used for sample)	
Step 1:		Cross-stitch (two strands)	
926	·		Ecru
9	−	760	Salmon
11	✕	3328	Salmon-med.
43	∴	815	Garnet-med.
266	▢	3347	Yellow Green-med. (two strands) +
		015HL	Chartreuse Balger high luster (1 strand)
244	⟋	987	Forest Green-dk. (two strands) +
		015HL	Chartreuse Balger high luster (1 strand)
905	+	645	Beaver Gray-vy. dk.
401	△	844	Beaver Gray-ultra dk.
400	○	414	Steel Gray-dk.
403	●	310	Black

Step 2: Couched Thread (two strands)

400		414	Steel Gray-dk.

FABRICS
Aida 11
Aida 14
Aida 18
Hardanger 22

DESIGN SIZES
11⅜" x 8⅛"
8⅞" x 6⅜"
7" x 5"
5⅝" x 4"

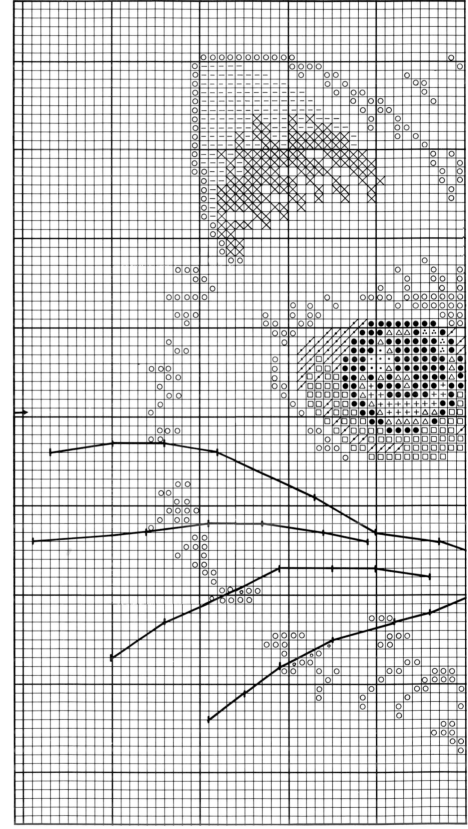

Stitch Count: 125 x 89

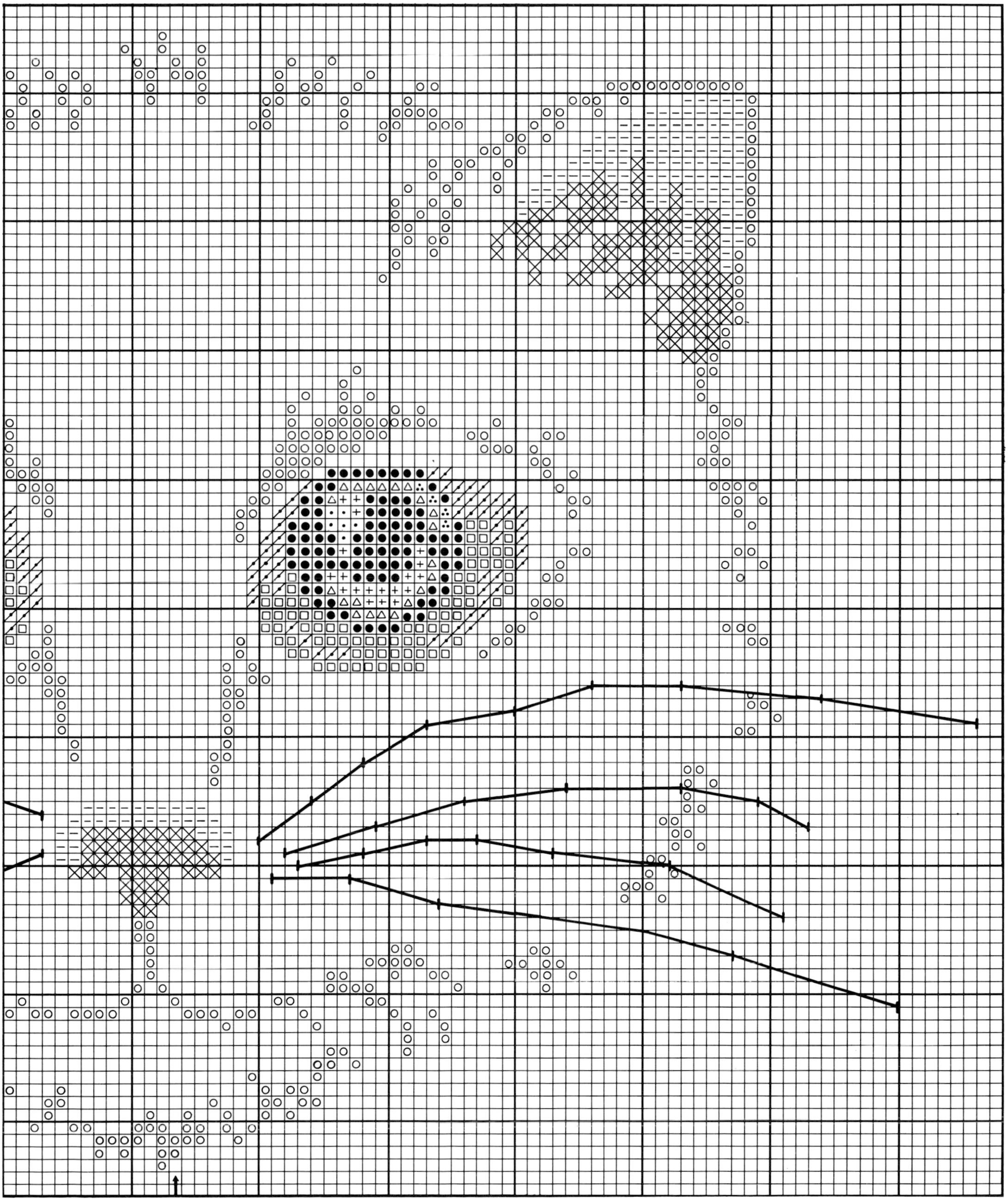

NOVEMBER 24
Thanksgiving

The Puritan settlers celebrated Thanksgiving instead of Christmas. Their religious beliefs as well as their difficult life in wild and unfamiliar country required discipline and sacrifice rather than gay and merry celebrations. The Pilgrims held a feast to express gratitude for their first successful harvest. Thanksgiving remains a day to gather together as families and welcome friends in a feeling of reverent thankfulness and reflection on the bounties and blessings of the past year.

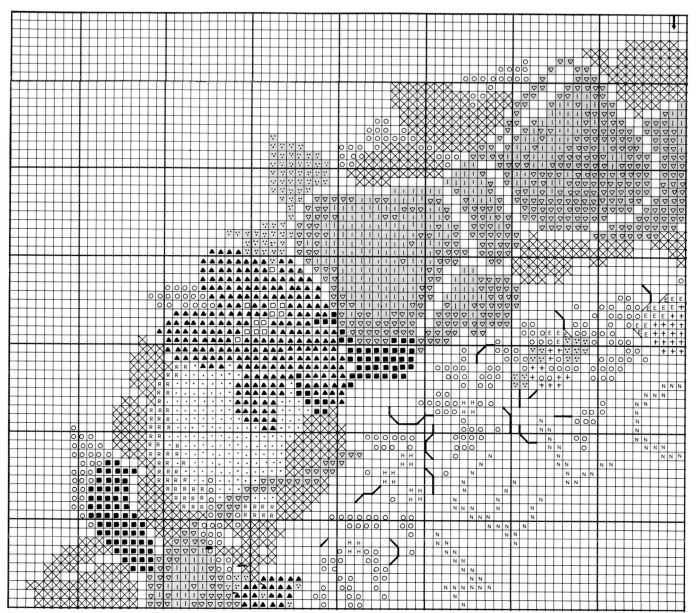

Stitch Count: 149 x 148

Welcome Wreath

SAMPLE

Stitched on cream Belfast Linen 32 over two threads, the finished design size is 9¼″ x 9¼″. The fabric was cut 16″ x 16″.

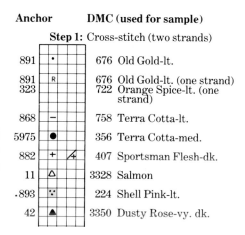

Anchor			DMC (used for sample)
			Step 1: Cross-stitch (two strands)
891	•		676 Old Gold-lt.
891	R		676 Old Gold-lt. (one strand)
323			722 Orange Spice-lt. (one strand)
868	−		758 Terra Cotta-lt.
5975	●		356 Terra Cotta-med.
882	+	◿	407 Sportsman Flesh-dk.
11	△		3328 Salmon
.893	⋰		224 Shell Pink-lt.
42	▲		3350 Dusty Rose-vy. dk.

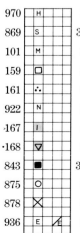

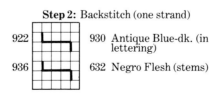

970	H		315	Antique Mauve-dk.
869	S		3042	Antique Violet-lt.
101	M		327	Antique Violet-dk.
159	□		827	Blue-vy. lt.
161	∴		826	Blue-med.
922	N		930	Antique Blue-dk.
·167	I		598	Turquoise-lt.
·168	▽		807	Peacock Blue
843	■		3364	Pine Green
875	O		503	Blue Green-med.
878	X		501	Blue Green-dk.
936	E		632	Negro Flesh

Step 2: Backstitch (one strand)

922		930	Antique Blue-dk. (in lettering)
936		632	Negro Flesh (stems)

FABRICS **DESIGN SIZES**
Aida 11 13½" x 13½"
Aida 14 10⅝" x 10⅝"
Aida 18 8¼" x 8¼"
Hardanger 22 6¾" x 6¾"

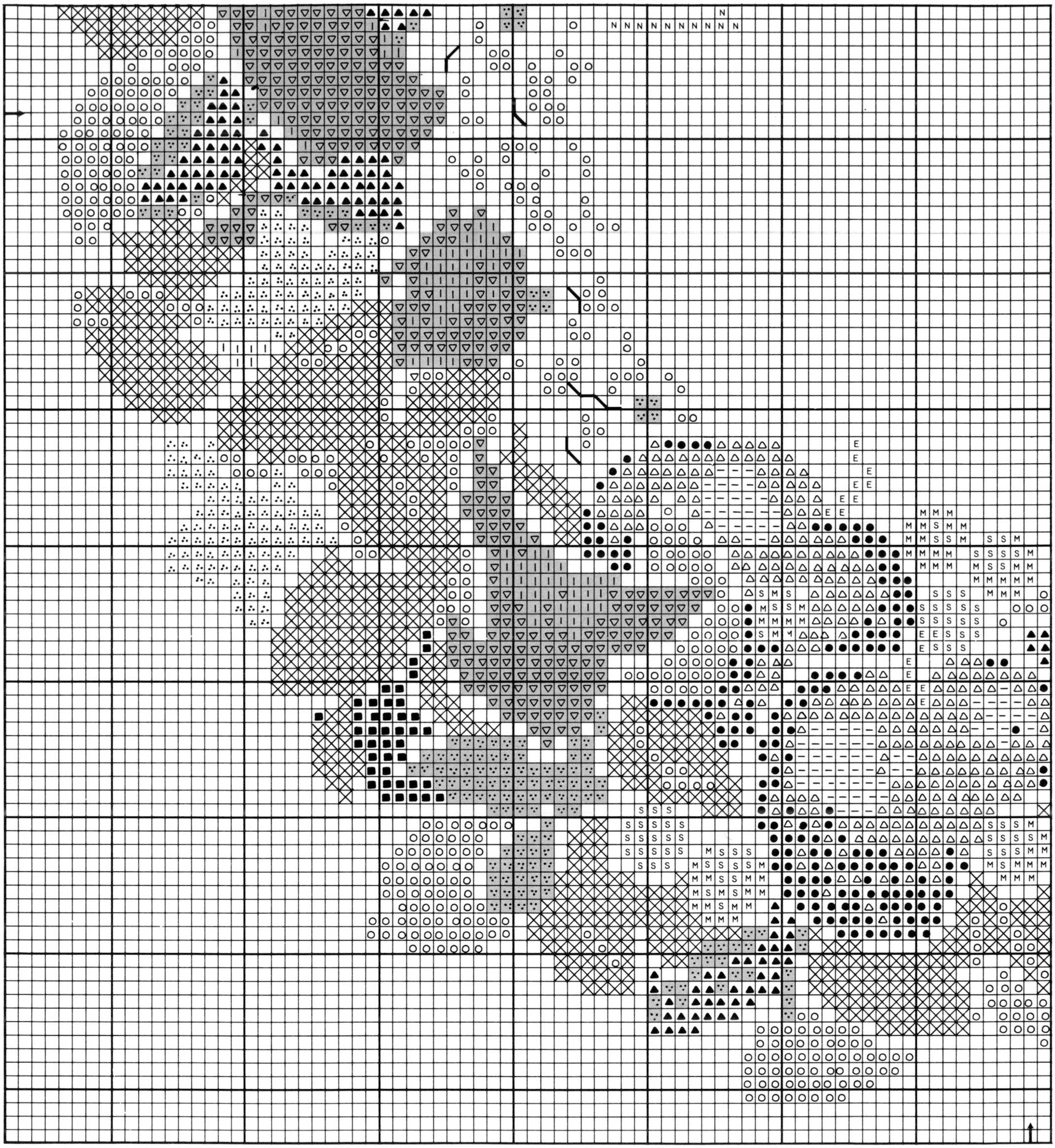

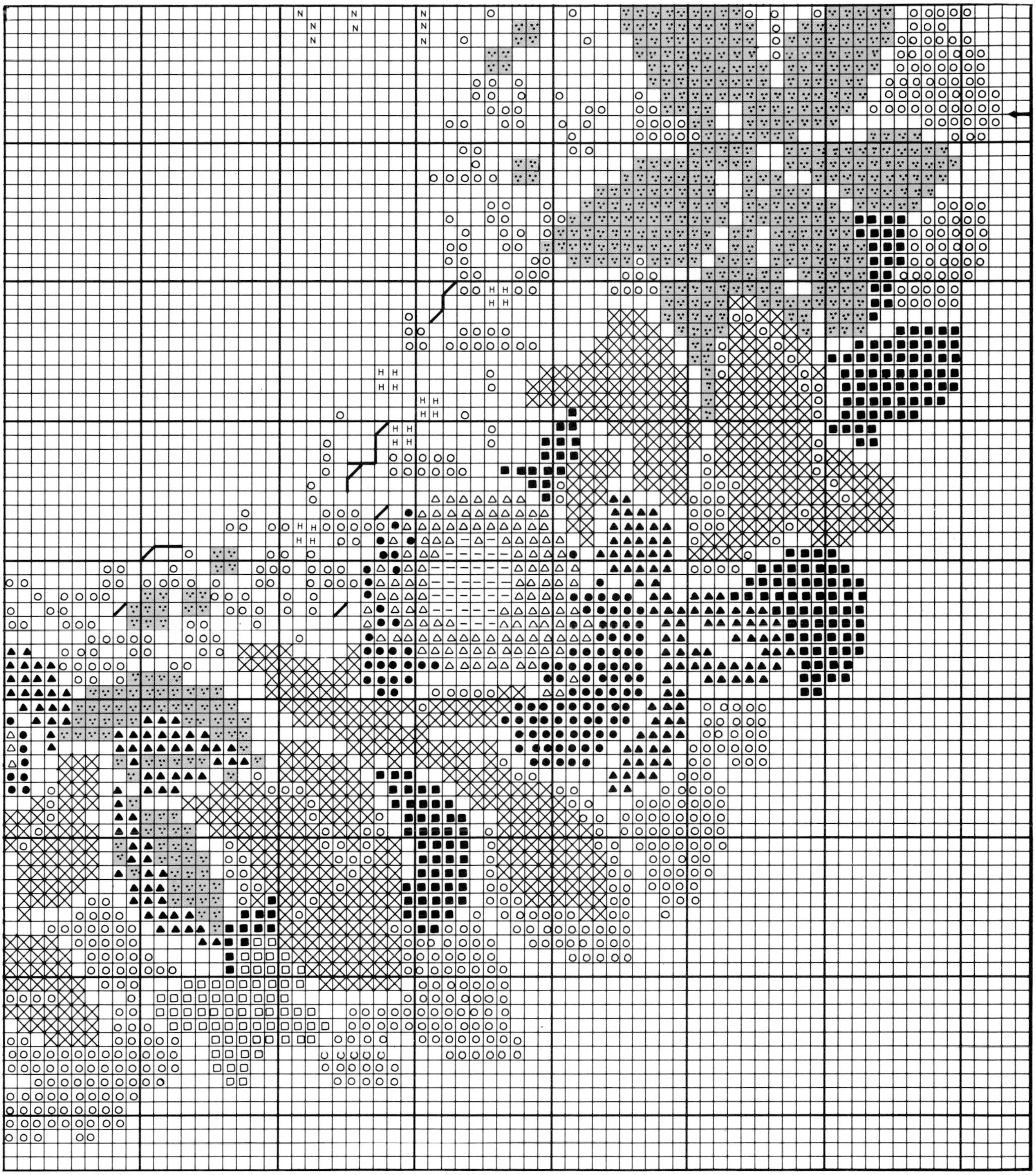

Window Cloth

SAMPLE

Stitched on ivory Belfast Linen 32 over two threads, the finished design size is 12¼" x 12¼". The fabric was cut 36" x 36". (See Step 1 of instructions for other sizes.) Begin stitching corner design 3" from each edge of fabric.

MATERIALS

Completed cross-stitch on ivory Belfast Linen 32
DMC ecru floss
Dressmakers' pen
Tweezers

DIRECTIONS

1. Measure length of curtain rod. Cut fabric according to chart below, placing design 2¼" from edges:

2. To prepare the stitched piece for hemstitching, find the center of one side of it. Mark the center 1¾" from the raw edge.

Beginning at the mark and moving down, withdraw four threads. To withdraw threads, using a pair of sharp, pointed embroidery scissors, carefully cut the horizontal threads at the mark and, with tweezers, gently pull threads from outside edges (Diagram A). Repeat with remaining sides. After drawing threads, press raw edge under ¼". Fold hem up so that top edge is even with bottom of drawn-thread area. Press. Pin and baste hem. Hemstitch across bottom of drawn-thread area, securing the folded edge of the hem in the stitching (Diagram B). Repeat on opposite edge; then, both sides.

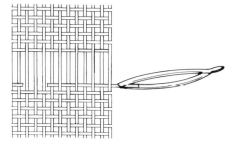

Diagram A

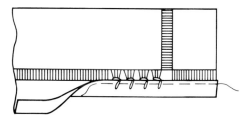

Diagram B

Trimmed Fabric Size	Rod Length	Finished Size
20" x 20"	24"	17" x 17"
22" x 22"	27"	19" x 19"
24" x 24"	30"	21" x 21"
26½" x 26½"	33"	23½" x 23½"
28½" x 28½"	36"	25½" x 25½"
30½" x 30½"	39"	27½" x 27½"
32½" x 32½"	42"	29½" x 29½"
35" x 35"	45"	32" x 32"

Anchor		DMC (used for sample)
Step 1: Cross-stitch (two strands)		
869	▼	3042 Antique Violet-lt.
842	O	3013 Khaki Green-lt.
859	X	3052 Gray Green-med.
Step 2: Backstitch (one strand)		
859	⌐	3052 Gray Green-med.

FABRICS	DESIGN SIZES
Aida 11	17¾" x 17⅞"
Aida 14	13⅞" x 14"
Aida 18	10⅞" x 10⅞"
Hardanger 22	8⅞" x 8⅞"

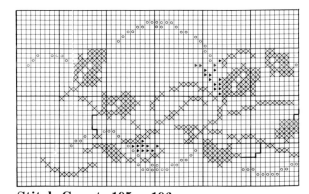

Stitch Count: 195 x 196

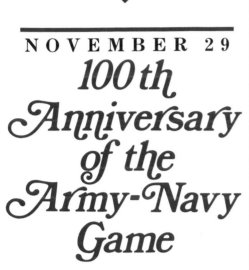

100th Anniversary of the Army-Navy Game

V-I-C-T-O-R-Y! For a century, American servicemen have gone head to head in an annual football showdown. The winners of the Commander-in-Chief's Trophy proudly display the coveted prize throughout the year until they meet again, vying to retain or regain this most sought-after award.

Army-Navy Game

SAMPLE
Stitched on aspen Aida 14, finished design size is 9⅜″ x 6⅜″. Fabric was cut 16″ x 13″.

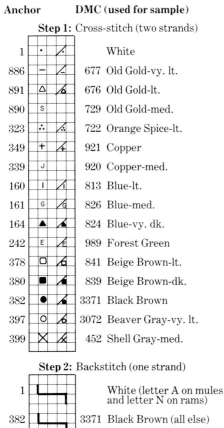

Anchor			DMC (used for sample)
Step 1:			Cross-stitch (two strands)
1	·	∕	White
886	−	∕	677 Old Gold-vy. lt.
891	△	∕	676 Old Gold-lt.
890	S		729 Old Gold-med.
323	∴	∕	722 Orange Spice-lt.
349	+	∕	921 Copper
339	J		920 Copper-med.
160	I	∕	813 Blue-lt.
161	G	∕G	826 Blue-med.
164	▲	∕	824 Blue-vy. dk.
242	E	∕E	989 Forest Green
378	□	∕	841 Beige Brown-lt.
380	■	∕	839 Beige Brown-dk.
382	●	∕	3371 Black Brown
397	O	∕	3072 Beaver Gray-vy. lt.
399	✕	∕	452 Shell Gray-med.

Step 2: Backstitch (one strand)

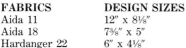

1		White (letter A on mules and letter N on rams)
382		3371 Black Brown (all else)

FABRICS

FABRICS	DESIGN SIZES
Aida 11	12″ x 8⅛″
Aida 18	7⅜″ x 5″
Hardanger 22	6″ x 4⅛″

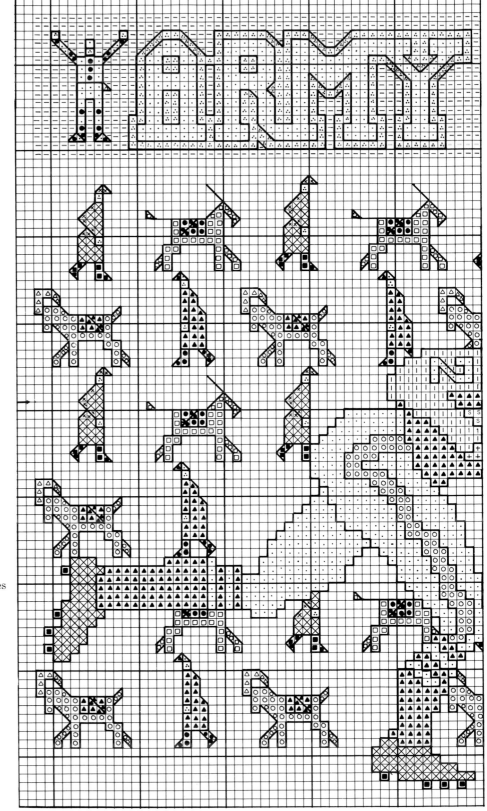

Stitch Count: 132 x 90

DECEMBER 24
Christmas Eve

In France, Christmas Eve is celebrated long into the night. Many families attend midnight Mass and, afterwards, sit down together for a festive holiday meal called "Le Reveillon." Then, with the same kind of joyous anticipation that children in America feel as they hang their stockings, French children place their shoes by the fireplace, hoping that Father Christmas, Père Noel, will fill them with many small gifts.

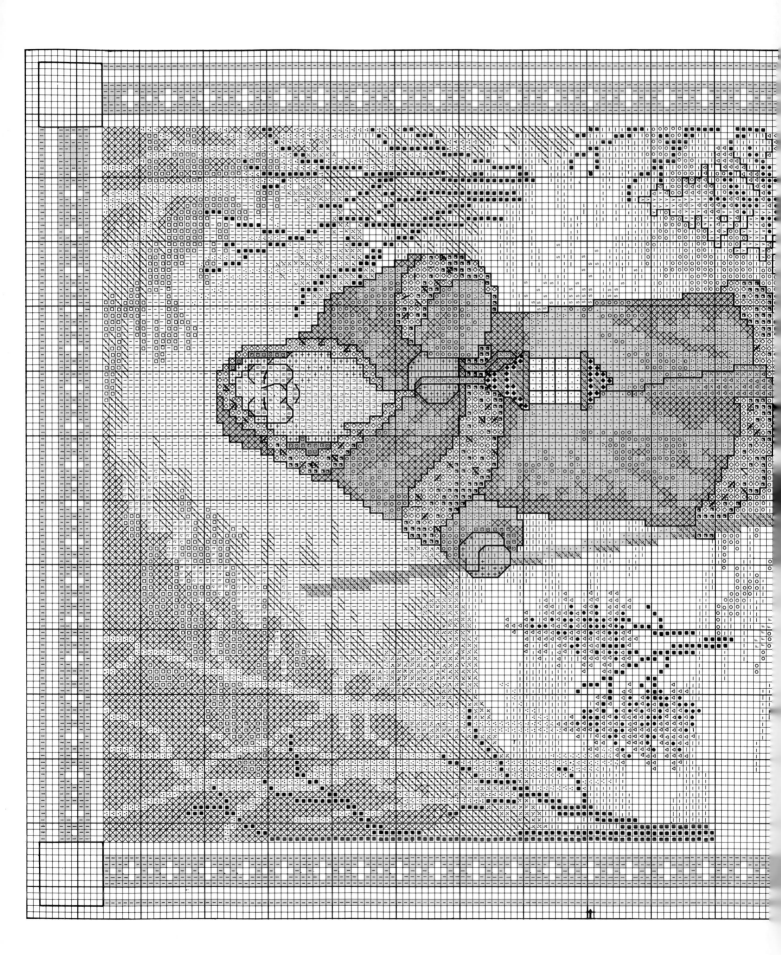

Stitch Count: 131 x 173

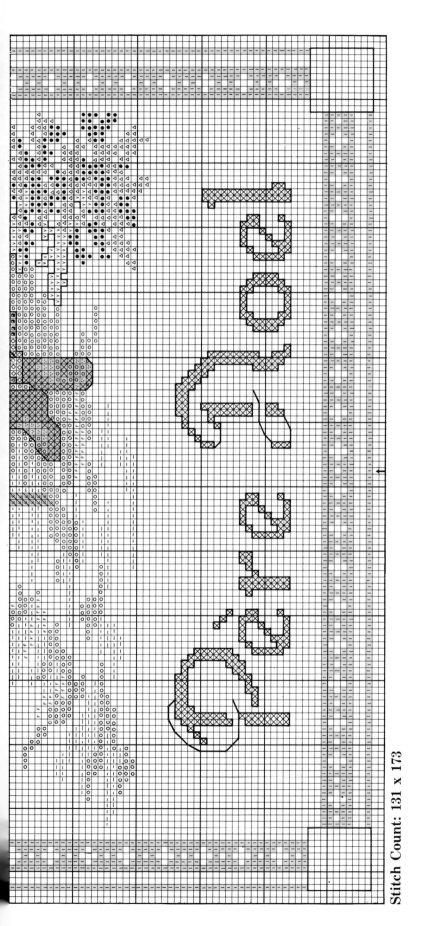

Père Noel

SAMPLE

Stitched on white Belfast Linen 32 over two threads, the finished design size is 8¼" x 10¾". The fabric was cut 15" x 17".

Anchor   DMC (used for sample)

Step 1: Cross-stitch (two strands)

1	∪	White
386	•	746 Off-white
289	s	307 Lemon
289 307 324 922	• ⁄	307 Lemon (one strand) + 922 Copper-lt. (one strand)
8	v	353 Peach Flesh
868	B	758 Terra-Cotta-lt.
324	–	922 Copper-lt.
349	+	921 Copper
339	o	920 Copper-med.
341	∴	919 Red Copper
341	X	918 Red Copper-dk.
893	✕	224 Shell Pink-lt.
894	◁	223 Shell Pink-med.
897	⊡	221 Shell Pink-dk.
117	F	341 Blue Violet-lt. (one strand)
117	F	341 Blue Violet-lt.
145	o	334 Baby Blue-med. (one strand)
145	☐	334 Baby Blue-med.
978	✕	322 Navy Blue-vy. lt.
920	–	932 Antique Blue-lt. (one strand)
920	–	932 Antique Blue-lt.
921	⁄	931 Antique Blue-med.
849	▬	927 Slate Green-med.
859	>	3053 Gray Green
859	ℵ	522 Fern Green
876	◁	502 Blue Green
878	✦	501 Blue Green-dk.
879	◈	500 Blue Green-vy. dk.
942	◇	738 Tan-vy. lt.
363	◨	436 Tan
307	◩	977 Golden Brown-lt.
308	◆	976 Golden Brown-med.
8581	+	3023 Brown Gray-lt.
898	∴	611 Drab Brown-dk.
889	■	610 Drab Brown-vy. dk.
397	z	3072 Beaver Gray-vy. lt.

Step 2: Backstitch (one strand)

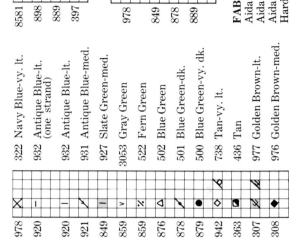

978	322 Navy Blue-vy. lt. (lettering)
849	927 Slate Green-med. (border)
878	501 Blue Green-dk. (tree)
889	610 Drab Brown-vy. dk. (all else)

DESIGN SIZES

Aida 11	11⅞" x 15¾"
Aida 14	9⅜" x 12⅜"
Aida 18	7¼" x 9⅝"
Hardanger 22	6" x 7⅞"

FABRICS

Christmas

Christmas traditions bring a continuity and wholeness to a family. Somehow the very sameness of the season provides much to look forward to and enough memories to carry through the year. These traditions, woven into the very pattern of our lives, are carried from generation to generation. Our lives are strengthened and enriched, because of these same simple Christmas routines and rituals.

Tree Skirt

SAMPLE

Stitched on white Jobelan 28 over two threads, the finished design size on each stocking for tree skirt is 2¾″ x 3½″. The fabric was cut 9″ x 9½″. Make eight designs.

MATERIALS

Completed cross-stitch on white Jobelan 28; matching thread

¼ yard of 45″-wide white Jobelan 28 (for stocking heels)

1½ yards of 45″-wide pink sport-weight fabric

¼ yard of 45″-wide light green fabric

¼ yard of 45″-wide pink print fabric

2 yards of 45″-wide white fabric for lining

4¼ yards of 45″-wide blue-green print fabric; matching thread

3 yards of ½″-wide blue-green satin ribbon

White acrylic paint

Small paintbrush

Mylar for stencil

Craft knife

Paper for pattern

Dressmakers' pen

DIRECTIONS

All seam allowances are ¼″.

1. Make pattern for stocking, transferring all details. Then cut the cuff off the pattern; set aside. Cut eight stockings from pink fabric, adding ¼″ seam allowance to the upper edge. Cut eight cuffs from green fabric, adding ¼″ seam allowance to the lower edge.

Cut the heel and toe off the pattern. Cut eight heel pieces from the unstitched Jobelan, adding ¼″ seam allowance to the inside edge. Center the toe pattern over each of the eight designs and cut out, adding ¼″ seam allowance to the inside edge. Cut eight ⅞″ x 6″ strips from pink print fabric.

2. Using a dressmakers' pen and referring to pattern for placement, mark the wavy lines on the right side of one stocking front. Using white thread, machine satin-stitch over the lines. Repeat for remaining stockings.

3. To make the floral stencil, trace and cut out flower pattern from mylar. Stencil flowers on stocking fronts with white paint (see photo for placement).

4. Mark placement for pink print strip on stocking. Fold under ¼″ on each long edge of the strip and slipstitch both edges to the stocking. Repeat with remaining strips and stockings. With right sides together and raw edges aligned, pin the bottom edge of one cuff piece to the top edge of one stocking. Stitch. Press seam toward stocking. Repeat with remaining stockings and cuff pieces.

5. Fold one design toe piece and one heel piece under ¼″ on inside edges. Place on stocking, matching outside raw edges. Slipstitch inside edges to stocking. Quilt ⅛″ inside slipstitched edges. Repeat with remaining stockings.

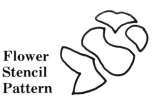

Flower Stencil Pattern

6. Using pieced stocking as a pattern, cut eight lining pieces from white fabric. With right sides together, pin one stocking to one stocking lining piece. Stitch around the entire stocking (including the top edge) leaving a small opening for turning. Clip curves and turn right side out. Slipstitch the opening closed. Repeat with remaining stockings.

7. Slipstitch the diagonal edge of one stocking cuff to the edge of another stocking as indicated on pattern. Repeat to connect the remaining stockings; do not connect the first and last stockings.

8. To make the tree skirt, cut the blue-green print fabric into three 45″ x 51″ pieces. Then cut one of the pieces in half to make two 22½″ x 51″ pieces. Pin one large piece to one small piece, right sides together and long edges aligned. Stitch on the long edge. Press seam open. Fold into quarters to find center; mark. Measure 3″ and 24″ from center and mark quarter circles (see Diagram). Cut on circle lines through the four layers of fabric. Then open skirt so that it is folded in half. Cut on one fold line from outside edge to center. This will be the center back opening.

Tree Skirt Pattern

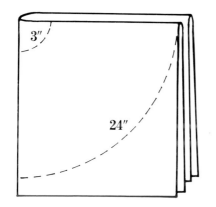

Diagram

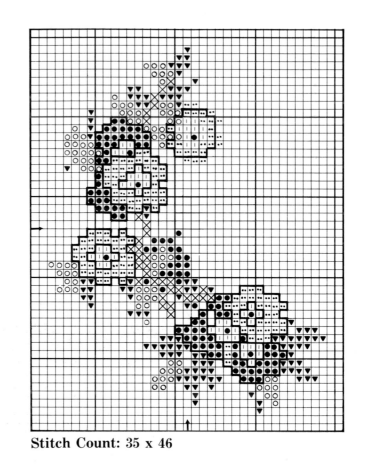

Stitch Count: 35 x 46

9. To make lining for skirt, repeat Step 8 with remaining two pieces of blue-green print fabric. Stitch the two circles with right sides together, leaving an opening for turning. Clip the curves. Turn right side out. Slipstitch the opening closed.

10. Place the connected stockings on skirt with toes of stockings 1″ from bottom edge of skirt (see photo). Baste to skirt. To attach stockings to skirt, stitch in-the-ditch at bottom edges of cuffs and at seams connecting stockings.

11. To attach ties, mark top, center, and bottom of both sides of opening of skirt. Cut ribbon into six pieces. Fold under one end of ribbon and tack the folded end securely at a mark. Repeat with remaining ribbon pieces, attaching them to the remaining marks.

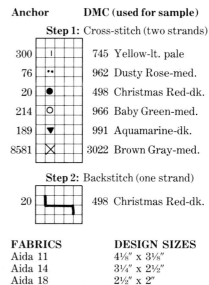

Anchor		DMC (used for sample)
	Step 1: Cross-stitch (two strands)	
300	I	745 Yellow-lt. pale
76	••	962 Dusty Rose-med.
20	●	498 Christmas Red-dk.
214	O	966 Baby Green-med.
189	▼	991 Aquamarine-dk.
8581	X	3022 Brown Gray-med.
	Step 2: Backstitch (one strand)	
20	⌐	498 Christmas Red-dk.

FABRICS	DESIGN SIZES
Aida 11	4⅛″ x 3⅛″
Aida 14	3¼″ x 2½″
Aida 18	2½″ x 2″
Hardanger 22	2⅛″ x 1⅝″

Tree Skirt Stocking Pattern
Each square = 1 inch.

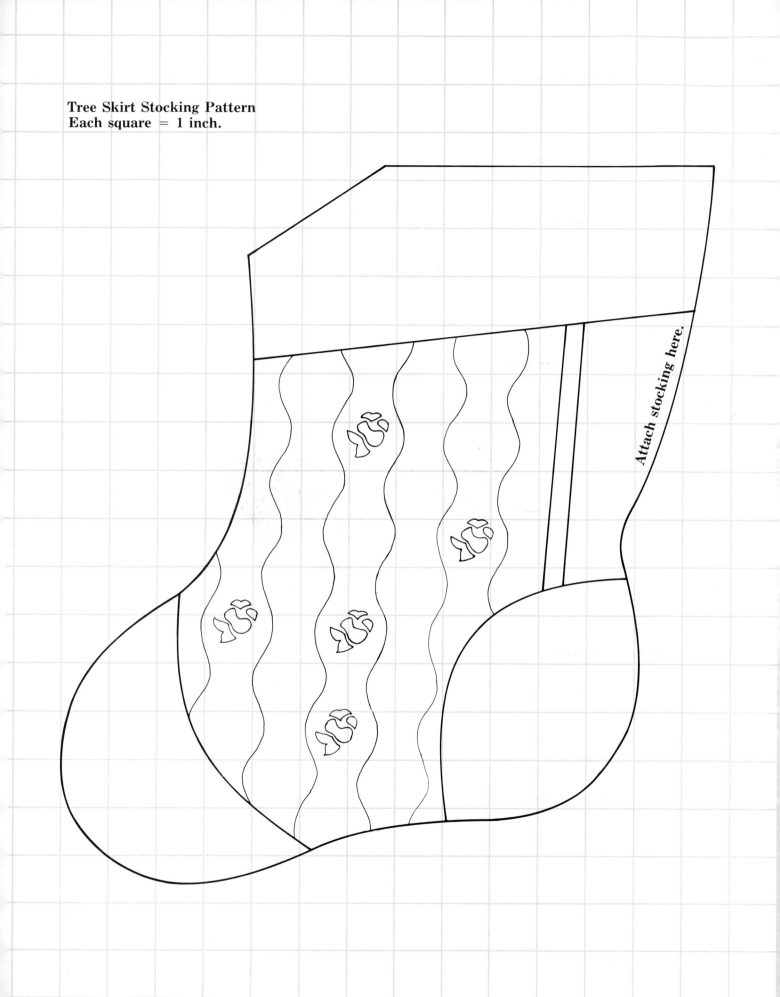

Attach stocking here.

Christmas Stocking

SAMPLE
Stitched on white Jobelan 28 over two threads, the finished design size is 6⅛″ x 10″. The fabric was cut 12″ x 20″.

MATERIALS
Completed cross-stitch on white Jobelan 28; matching thread
½ yard of blue-green fabric; matching thread
½ yard of muslin
½ yard of polyester fleece
1¾ yards of ⅝″-wide pink satin ribbon
DMC 747 embroidery floss
Paper for pattern
Dressmakers' pen

DIRECTIONS
All seam allowances are ¼″.

1. Make pattern for stocking, transferring all markings. Also make a pattern for flower embroidery motif.

2. From blue-green fabric, cut four stocking pieces and one 2½″ x 20″ strip for ruffle. Cut two stocking pieces from polyester fleece and one from muslin.

3. To make a pattern for design piece, draw a straight line across the top of the stocking pattern, 1″ below the edge. Next draw a line all around the rest of the stocking pattern, 1¼″ inside the edge. Cut along this line. Place pattern over the design piece with the top edge of pattern ½″ above the top edge of the design. Cut out.

4. Turn the raw edges of the cross-stitched stocking under ¼″. Center it on the fabric stocking front and slipstitch in place.

5. Beginning in the top left corner of the stocking front, trace the flower motif with the dressmakers' pen. Then trace 14 more motifs, 1¼″ apart, around the outside edge of stocking (see photo). Using DMC 747 floss, satin-stitch each motif.

6. Layer the muslin, fleece, and the stocking front (right side up). Baste, securing the three layers. Baste the second piece of fleece to the wrong side of the stocking back.

7. Using blue-green thread, quilt in-the-ditch on the blue-green

stocking around the cross-stitched stocking and the embroidered flowers. Then echo-quilt ⅜″, ½″, and ⅝″ outside the first quilting line, except where embroidered flowers are. Quilt toe lines according to pattern. With white thread, quilt ⅛″ inside cross-stitched white diamonds.

8. Fold the ruffle piece with right sides together, to measure 1¼″ x 20″. Stitch the ends. Turn right side out. Run a gathering thread close to the raw edges. Gather to fit the top edge of the stocking front. With right sides together and raw edges aligned, pin the ruffle to the top edge of the stocking. Stitch.

9. Pin the right sides of the stocking front and back together.

Stitch, leaving top open and catching the fleece in seams. Trim the fleece from seam allowance. Clip the curves and turn right side out.

10. Sew the lining pieces, with right sides together, leaving top open and an opening for turning. Clip the curves. Do not turn. Slide the lining over the stocking, with right sides together, side seams matching, and the ruffle tucked inside. Stitch around the top edge of the stocking. Turn the stocking through the opening in lining. Slipstitch the opening closed.

11. Cut a 6¾″ piece of ribbon. Lay it along the top edge of cross-stitched stocking, covering ¼″ of stocking. Slipstitch both edges of ribbon to stocking. Cut the re-

maining ribbon in half. Fold one piece into two 5″ loops. Then fold the looped piece in half and tack to one corner of attached ribbon. Repeat with second ribbon piece, tacking it to the opposite corner.

Embroidery Pattern

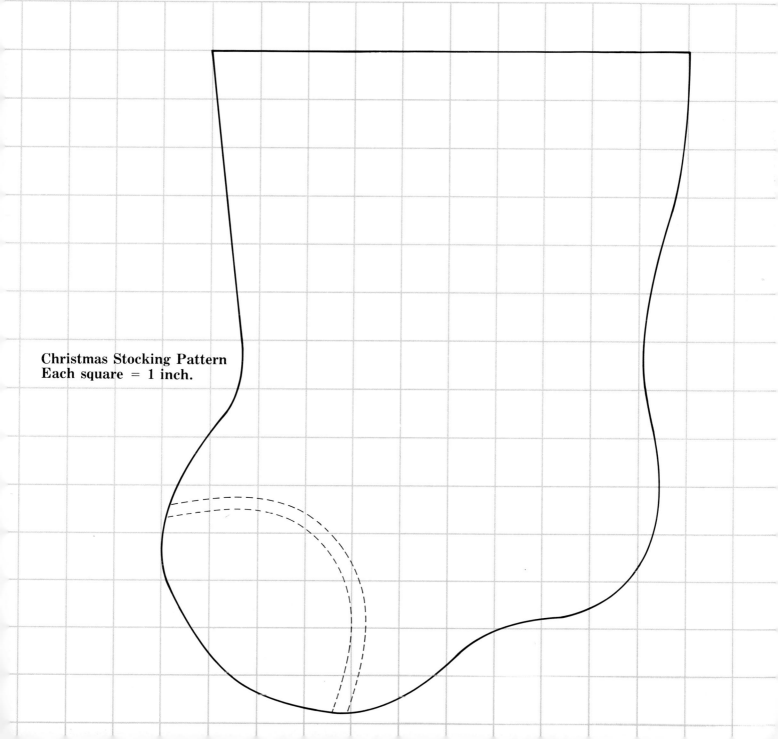

Christmas Stocking Pattern
Each square = 1 inch.

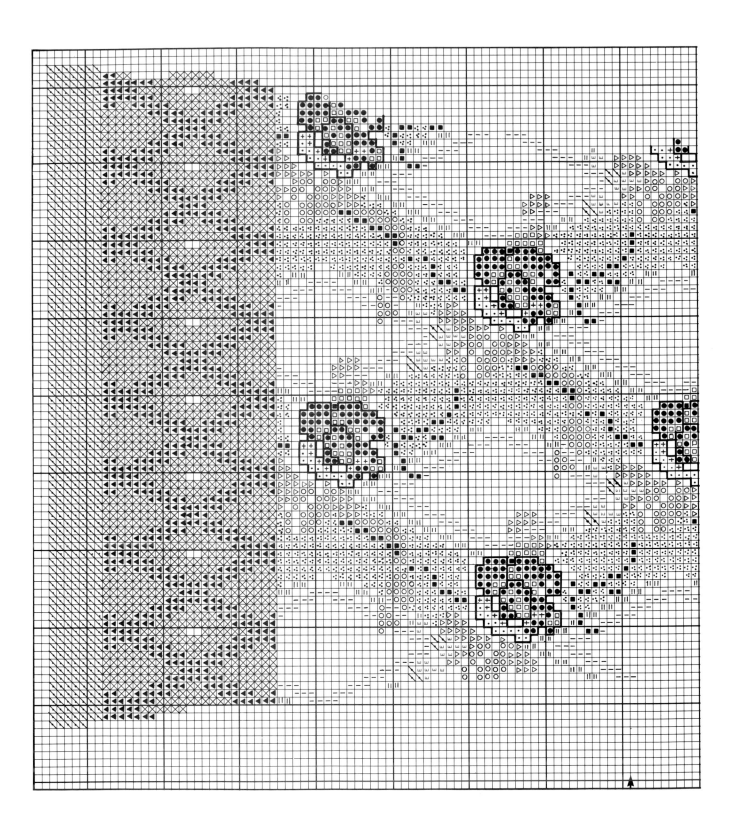

Stitch Count: 92 x 152

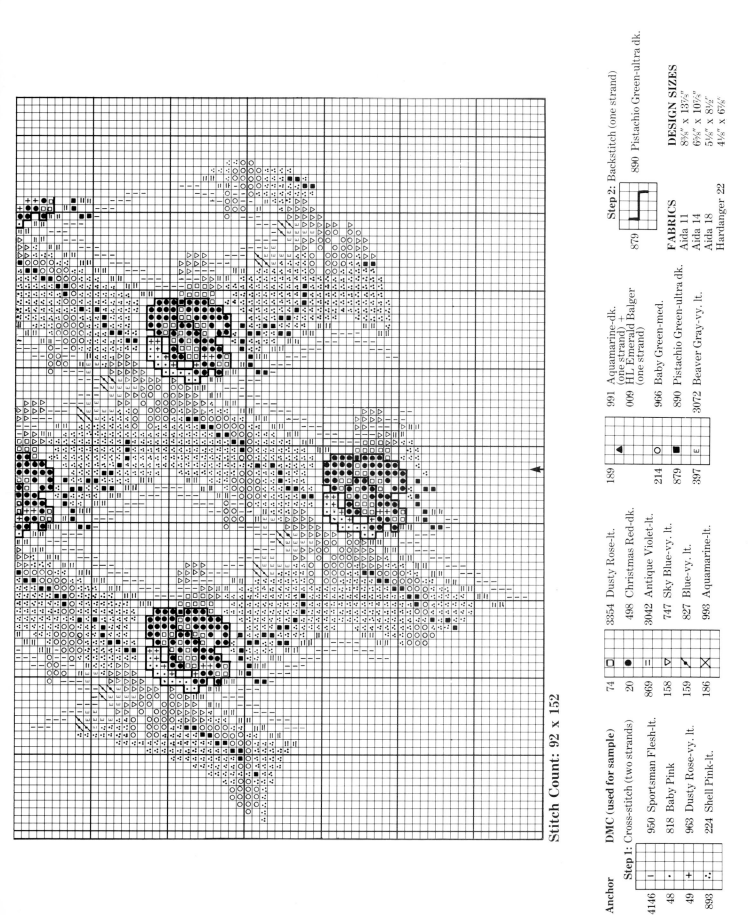

133

Anchor		DMC (used for sample)
	Step 1:	Cross-stitch (two strands)
4146	I	950 Sportsman Flesh-lt.
48	·	818 Baby Pink
49	+	963 Dusty Rose-vy. lt.
893	∴	224 Shell Pink-lt.
74	▢	3354 Dusty Rose-lt.
20	●	498 Christmas Red-dk.
869	II	3042 Antique Violet-lt.
158	▷	747 Sky Blue-vy. lt.
159	◢	827 Blue-vy. lt.
186	✕	993 Aquamarine-lt.
189	◀	991 Aquamarine-dk.
		009 HL Emerald Balger (one strand) + (one strand)
214	○	966 Baby Green-med.
879	■	890 Pistachio Green-ultra dk.
397	E	3072 Beaver Gray-vy. lt.

Step 2: Backstitch (one strand)

879	
	890 Pistachio Green-ultra dk.

DESIGN SIZES

FABRICS	
Aida 11	8⅜" x 13⅞"
Aida 14	6⅝" x 10⅞"
Aida 18	5⅛" x 8½"
Hardanger 22	4⅛" x 6⅞"

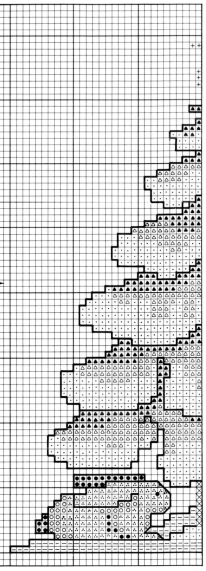

Stitch Count: 125 x 83

Merry Christmas

SAMPLE
Stitched on white Aida 14 over one thread, finished design size is 8⅞" x 5⅞". Fabric was cut 15" x 12".

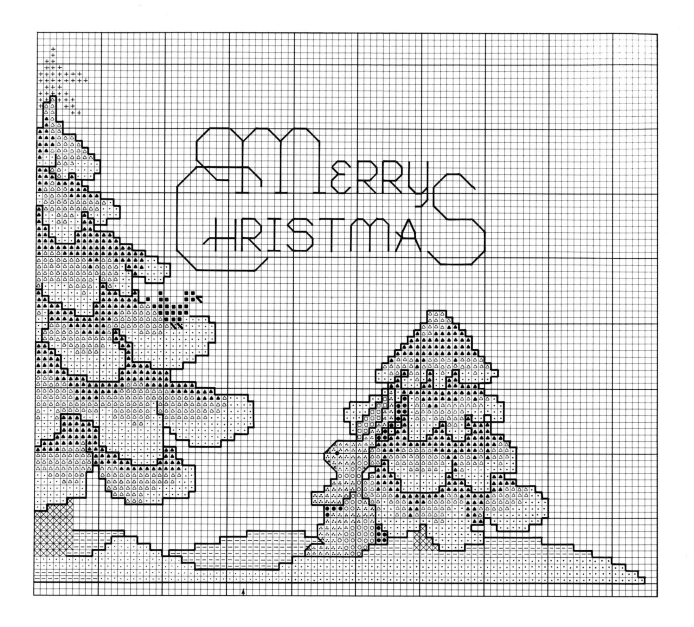

Anchor	DMC (used for sample)		
Step 1: Cross-stitch (two strands)			
1	·		White
297	+		743 Yellow-med.
24	▢		776 Pink-med.
158	−	⟋	775 Baby Blue-lt.
131	■		798 Delft-dk.
209	△		913 Nile Green-med.
228	▲		910 Emerald Green-dk.
371	✕		433 Brown-med.
398	⋰	⟋	415 Pearl Gray
400	○	◿	414 Steel Gray-dk.
401	●		413 Pewter Gray-dk.

Step 2: Backstitch (one strand)

47		321 Christmas Red (lettering)
131		798 Delft-dk. (bird, snow on ground)
879		890 Pistachio Green-ultra dk. (trees)
401		413 Pewter Gray-dk. (rabbits)

Step 3: French knots (one strand)

401	●	413 Pewter Gray-dk.

FABRICS	DESIGN SIZES
Aida 11	11⅜″ x 7½″
Aida 18	7″ x 4⅝″
Hardanger 22	5⅝″ x 3¾″

Manger Stocking

SAMPLE
Stitched on white Hardanger 22 over two threads, the finished design size is 10″ x 13¼″. The fabric was cut 14″ x 18″.

MATERIALS
Completed cross-stitch on white Hardanger 22
⅜ yard of burgundy velvet fabric; matching thread
½ yard of burgundy satin fabric
One 14″ x 18″ piece of polyester fleece
½ yard of gold looped fringe
1 yard of ¼″-diameter twisted multicolored cording
2 yards of ¾″-diameter twisted burgundy cording (available with drapery supplies)
Paper for pattern
Dressmakers' pen

DIRECTIONS
All seam allowances are ¼″.

1. Make pattern for stocking.

2. For stocking front, place the top edge of pattern 3″ above the top of the stitched design piece and cut out.

3. From the burgundy velvet, cut one stocking piece for backing. Cut two stocking pieces from burgundy satin for lining. Cut one from polyester fleece.

4. Cut two 8½″ pieces of gold fringe. Stitch a strip of fringe across the stocking top, 1¼″ above the stitched design, and the second strip 2¼″ above the design.

5. Baste the fleece to wrong side of stocking front. Then, with right sides together, stitch the stocking front to the back, leaving top open. Be sure to catch fleece in the seams. Clip the curves. Turn right side out.

6. With right sides together, sew the lining pieces together, leaving the top open and an opening in the side seam for turning. Clip the curves. Do not turn right side out.

7. Slide the lining over stocking, with right sides together and side seams matching. Stitch around the top edge of the stocking. Turn the stocking through opening in lining. Slipstitch opening closed.

8. Tuck the lining inside the stocking. By hand, tack the lining to the side seam allowances.

9. Cut an 8½″ piece of ¼″ cording. Cover the straight edge of the lower strip of gold fringe on the stocking front with this piece; slipstitch across and secure at each side seam.

10. Slipstitch ¾″ cording around stocking, beginning at the top right of the stocking back. Stitch cording across the top and down the left side, around the toe, up the right side, and across the top of the front. (See photo.) Cut the cording, leaving an 8″ tail.

11. Cut a 22″ piece of ¼″ cording. Fold the cording in half and slipstitch the fold to the the top right side seam (with stocking front facing you). Unwind the cording into its separate strands, knotting each strand 2″ from the end to prevent unraveling.

12. Make a 2½″ loop with the 8″ tail of the ¾″ cording and secure the loop by tying it with the ¼″ cording. Fray the remaining 3″ tail of the ¾″ cording.

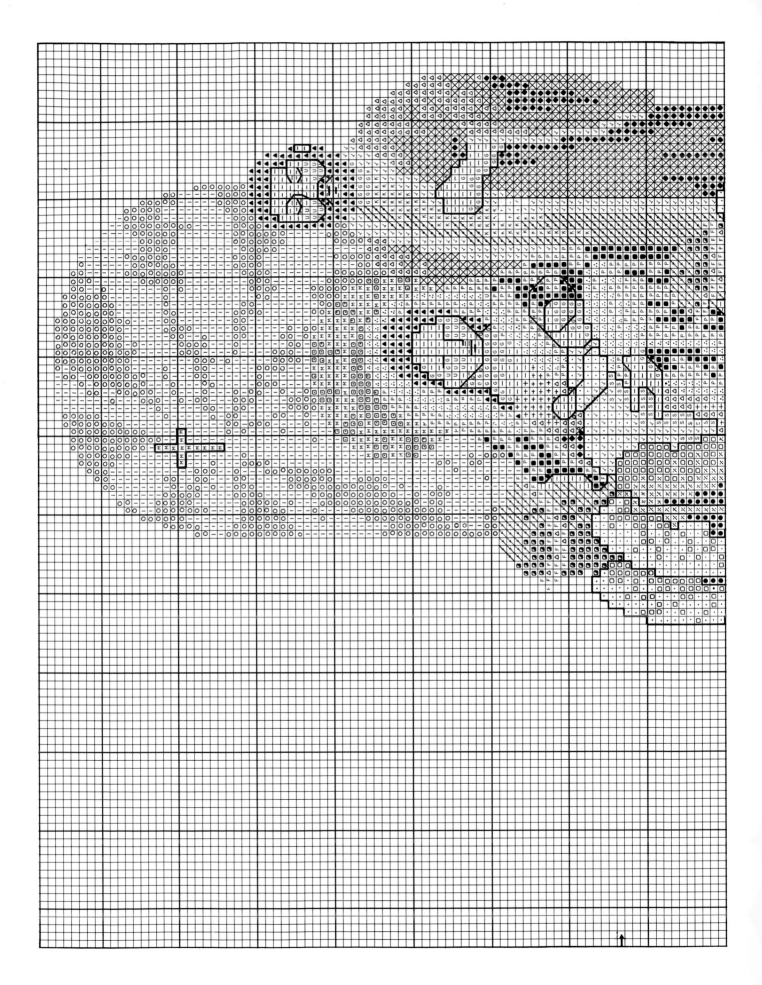

Stitch Count: 111 x 145

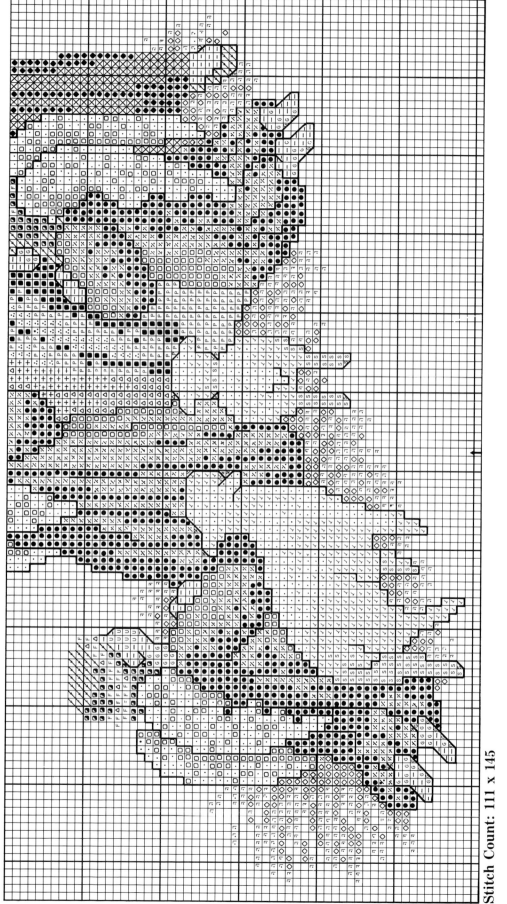

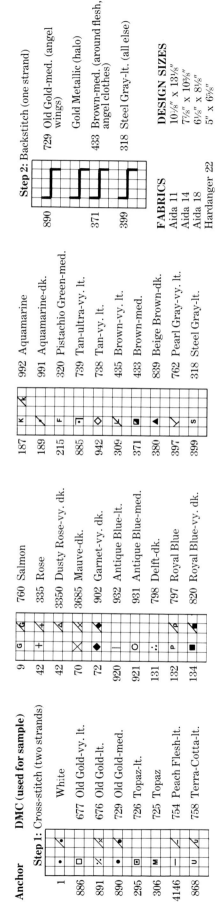

Anchor		DMC (used for sample)

Step 1: Cross-stitch (two strands)

1	•	⟋	White
886		□	677 Old Gold-vy. lt.
891	×	⟋	676 Old Gold-lt.
890	●	◢	729 Old Gold-med.
295	⊡		726 Topaz-lt.
306	M		725 Topaz
4146	−	⟋	754 Peach Flesh-lt.
868	U	⟍	758 Terra-Cotta-lt.

9	G	G	760 Salmon
42	+	◮	335 Rose
42		⟍	3350 Dusty Rose-vy. dk.
70		⨯	3685 Mauve-dk.
72		◆	902 Garnet-vy. dk.
920		▮	932 Antique Blue-lt.
921	◻	O	931 Antique Blue-med.
131		⠂⠂	798 Delft-dk.
132	P	◿	797 Royal Blue
134		■	820 Royal Blue-vy. dk.

187		K	K	992 Aquamarine
189			⟋	991 Aquamarine-dk.
215		F		320 Pistachio Green-med.
885		⊡	◇	739 Tan-ultra-vy. lt.
942			◿	738 Tan-vy. lt.
309				435 Brown-vy. lt.
371			▪	433 Brown-med.
380			▲	839 Beige Brown-dk.
397			⟍	762 Pearl Gray-vy. lt.
399		s		318 Steel Gray-lt.

Step 2: Backstitch (one strand)

890		729 Old Gold-med. (angel wings)
		Gold Metallic (halo)
371		433 Brown-med. (around flesh, angel clothes)
399		318 Steel Gray-lt. (all else)

DESIGN SIZES
10⅛" x 13⅛"
7⅞" x 10⅜"
6⅛" x 8⅛"
5" x 6⅝"

FABRICS
Aida 11
Aida 14
Aida 18
Hardanger 22

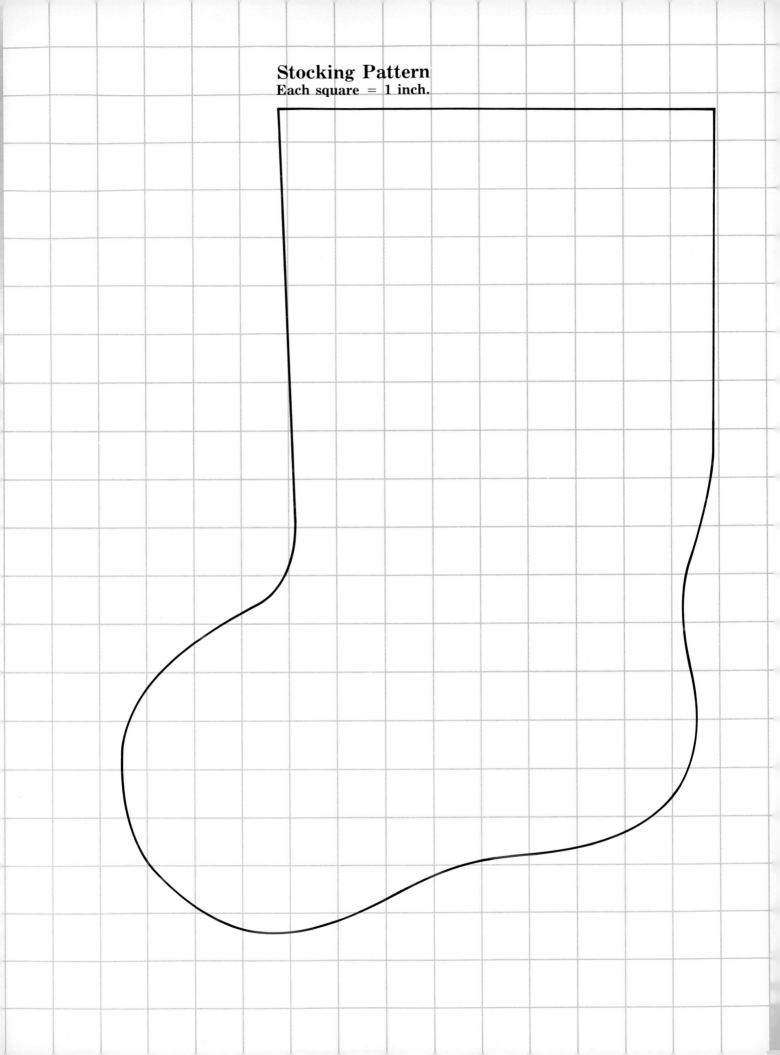

Stocking Pattern
Each square = 1 inch.

General Instructions

Cross-Stitch

Fabrics: Counted cross-stitch is usually worked on even-weave fabric. These fabrics are manufactured specifically for counted thread embroidery and are woven with the same number of vertical as horizontal threads per inch. Because the number of threads in the fabric is equal in each direction, each stitch will be the same size. It is the number of threads per inch in even-weave fabrics that determines the size of a finished design.

Preparing Fabric: Cut even-weave fabric at least 3″ larger on all sides than the design size or cut it the size specified in the sample paragraph. A 3″ margin is the minimum amount of space that allows for working the edges of the design comfortably. To keep fabric from fraying, whipstitch or machine-zigzag the raw edges.

Needles: Needles should slip easily through the holes in the fabric but not pierce the fabric. Use a blunt tapestry needle, size 24 or 26. Never leave the needle in the design area of your work. It can leave rust or a permanent impression on your fabric.

Finished Design Size: To determine the finished size of a design, divide the stitch count by the threads per inch of the fabric. When designs are stitched over two threads, divide the stitch count by half the threads per inch.

Hoop or Frame: Select a hoop or stretcher bars large enough to hold the entire design. Place the screw or the clamp of the hoop in a 10 o'clock position (or 2 o'clock, if you are left-handed) to keep from catching the thread.

Floss: All numbers and color names are cross-referenced between Anchor and DMC brands of six-strand embroidery floss. Cut 18″ lengths of floss. Run the floss over a damp sponge to straighten. Separate all six strands and use the number of strands called for in the code.

Centering Design: Find the center of the fabric by folding it in half horizontally and then vertically. Place a pin in the point of the fold to mark the center. Locate the center of the design on the graph by following the vertical and horizontal arrows. Begin stitching at center points of graph and fabric.

Securing Floss: Start by inserting your needle up from the underside of the fabric. Hold 1″ of thread behind the fabric and stitch over it, securing it with the first few stitches. To secure thread when finishing, run needle under four or more stitches on the back of the design. Never knot floss unless working on clothing.

Another method for securing floss is the waste knot. Knot your floss and insert your needle from the right side of the fabric about 1″ from the design area. Work several stitches over the thread to secure. Cut off the knot later.

Stitching Method: For a smooth cross-stitch, use the push-and-pull method. Push the needle straight down and completely through the fabric before pulling it back up again. Do not pull the thread tight.

The tension should be consistent throughout, making the stitches even. Make one stitch for every symbol on the chart. To stitch in rows, work from left to right and then back.

Carrying Floss: To carry floss, weave floss under the previously worked stitches on the back. Do not carry your thread across any fabric that is not or will not be stitched. Loose threads, especially dark ones, will show through the fabric.

Twisted Floss: If floss is twisted, drop the needle and allow the floss to unwind itself. Floss will cover best when lying flat. Use thread no longer than 18″ because it will tend to twist and knot.

Cleaning Completed Work: When all stitching is complete, soak the completed work in cold water with a mild soap for 5 to 10 minutes. Rinse and roll work in a towel to remove excess water; do not wring. Place work face down on a dry towel and, with iron on warm setting, iron until work is dry.

Beadwork

Attach beads to fabric with a half-cross, lower left to upper right. Secure beads by returning thread through beads, lower right to upper left. Complete row of half-crosses before returning to secure all beads.

Stitches

Cross-stitch: Make one cross for each symbol on the chart. Bring needle and thread up at A, down at B, up at C, and down again at D (Diagram A). For rows, stitch from left to right, then back (Diagram B). All stitches should lie in the same direction.

Diagram A

Diagram B

Half-cross: Make the longer stitch in the direction of the slanted line on the graph. The stitch actually fills three-fourths of the area. Bring needle and thread up at A, down at B, up at C, and down at D (Diagram C).

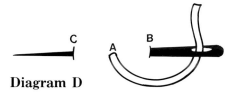

Diagram C

Backstitch: Complete all cross-stitching before working back stitches or other accent stitches. Working from left to right with one strand of floss (unless indicated otherwise in code), bring needle and thread up at A, down at B, and up again at C. Going back down at A, continue in this manner (Diagram D).

Diagram D

French Knot: Bring needle up at A, using one strand of floss. Wrap floss around needle two times (unless indicated otherwise in instructions). Insert needle beside A, pulling floss until it fits snugly around needle. Pull needle through to back (Diagram E).

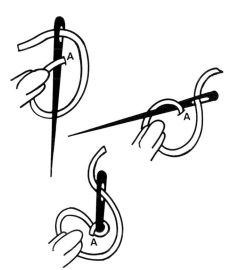

Diagram E

WASTE CANVAS

Cut the waste canvas 1″ larger on all sides than the finished design. Baste the waste canvas to the fabric to be stitched. Complete the stitching; each stitch is over one unit (two threads). When stitching is complete, use a spray bottle to dampen the stitched area with cold water. Pull the waste canvas threads out one at a time with tweezers. It is easier to pull all the threads running in one direction first; then pull out the opposite threads. Allow the stitching to dry; then place face down on a towel and iron.

Sewing Hints

Bias Strips: Bias strips are used for ruffles, binding, or corded piping. To cut bias strips, fold the fabric at a 45-degree angle to the grain of the fabric and crease. Cut on the crease. Cut additional strips the width indicated in instructions and parallel to the first cutting line. The ends of the bias strips should be on the grain of the fabric. Place the right sides of the ends together and stitch with ¼″ seam. Continue to piece strips until they are the length indicated in instructions (Diagram F).

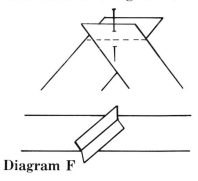

Diagram F

Slipstitch: Insert needle at A, slide it through the folded edge of the fabric for about ⅛″ to ¼″ and bring it out at B. Directly below B, take a small stitch through the second piece of fabric (Diagram G).

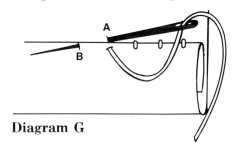

Diagram G

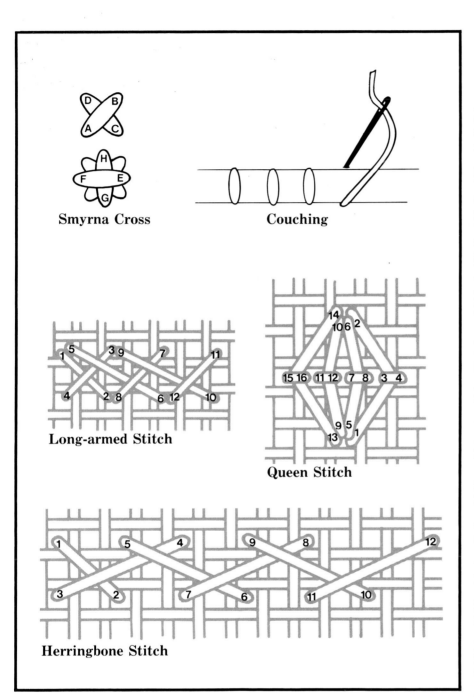

Smyrna Cross

Couching

Long-armed Stitch

Queen Stitch

Herringbone Stitch

All products are available retail from Shepherd's Bush, 220 24th Street, Ogden, UT 84401; (801) 399-4546; or for a merchant near you, write the following suppliers:

Zweigart Fabrics—Zweigart/Joan Toggitt Ltd., Weston Canal Plaza, 2 Riverview Drive, Somerset, NJ 08873

Zweigart Fabrics used:

White Aida 14	Cream Rimini 27
Cream Aida 14	White Linda 27
Spun Straw Aida 14	Cream Linda 27
Waste Canvas 14	White Belfast Linen 32
White Hardanger 22	Cream Belfast Linen 32
Moss Lugana 25	Driftwood Belfast Linen 32
Navy Lugana 25	Ivory Belfast Linen 32

Aspen Aida 14, Natural Super Linen 28—Charles Craft, P.O. Box 1049, Laurinburg, NC 28352

Pistachio Aida 14, Toasted Rye Ragusa 14, White Jobelan 28—Wichelt Imports, Inc., Rural Route 1, Stoddard, WI 54658

Light Brown Linen 26—Craft World, P.O. Box 779, New Windsor, MD 21776

Brown Perforated Paper 14—Astor Place, 239 Main Avenue, Stirling, NJ 07980

Cream Rimini 27—Chapelle Designers, P.O. Box 9252, Newgate Station, Ogden, UT 84409

White/Blue Waffle Towel—Norden Crafts, P.O. Box 1, Glenview, IL 60025

Fireplace Screen—Plain 'n' Fancy, P.O. Box 357, Mathews, VA 23109

Porcelain Jar (#PL1), Locket (#01)—Anne Brinkley Designs, 21 Ransom Road, Newton Centre, MA 02159

Beads—Gay Bowles Sales, Inc., 1310 Plainfield Ave., Janesville, WI 53547

Satin Ribbon—C.M. Offray & Sons, Rt. 24, Box 201, Chester, NJ 07930-0601

Silk Ribbon—Y.L.I. Corp., 45 W. 300 No., Provo, UT 84601

Balger Products—Kreinik Mfg. Co., Inc., 1708 Gihon Road, Parkersburg, WV 26101

Jacket Motifs

Pumpkin

Anchor			DMC (used for sample)
Step 1: Cross-stitch (two strands)			
323	–	╱	722 Orange Spice-lt.
324	O	◸	721 Orange Spice-med.
47	□	◸	321 Christmas Red
20	●	◢	498 Christmas Red-dk.
98	·		553 Violet-med.
99	▲		552 Violet-dk.
88	+		718 Plum
257	△		3346 Hunter Green
371	■		433 Brown-med.

Anchor		DMC (used for sample)
Step 2: Backstitch (one strand)		
212		561 Jade-vy. dk. (vine)
382		3371 Black Brown (grapes)

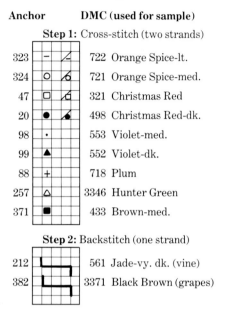

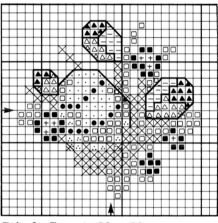

Stitch Count: 20 x 24

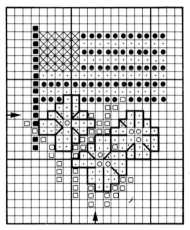

Stitch Count: 18 x 23

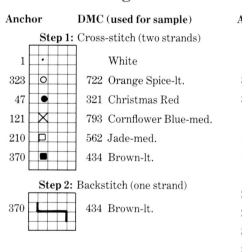

Stitch Count: 23 x 22

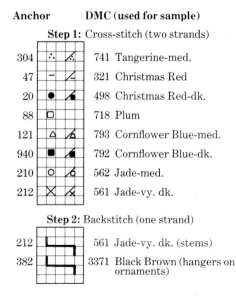

Stitch Count: 23 x 22

Flag

Anchor		DMC (used for sample)
Step 1: Cross-stitch (two strands)		
1	·	White
323	O	722 Orange Spice-lt.
47	●	321 Christmas Red
121	✕	793 Cornflower Blue-med.
210	□	562 Jade-med.
370	■	434 Brown-lt.

Anchor		DMC (used for sample)
Step 2: Backstitch (one strand)		
370		434 Brown-lt.

Eggs

Anchor			DMC (used for sample)
Step 1: Cross-stitch (two strands)			
1	·	╱	White
303	+		742 Tangerine-lt.
316	●	◢	740 Tangerine
76	■		603 Cranberry
108	–	╱	211 Lavender-lt.
104	△	◸	210 Lavender-med.
99	▲	◸	552 Violet-dk.
203	O	◸	564 Jade-vy. lt.
210	✕	◸	562 Jade-med.
397	□	◸	762 Pearl Gray-vy. lt.
398	∴	◸	415 Pearl Gray

Anchor		DMC (used for sample)
Step 2: Backstitch (one strand)		
400		317 Pewter Gray

Ornaments

Anchor			DMC (used for sample)
Step 1: Cross-stitch (two strands)			
304	∴	◸	741 Tangerine-med.
47	–	╱	321 Christmas Red
20	●	◢	498 Christmas Red-dk.
88	□		718 Plum
121	△	◸	793 Cornflower Blue-med.
940	■	◢	792 Cornflower Blue-dk.
210	O	◸	562 Jade-med.
212	✕	◸	561 Jade-vy. dk.

Anchor		DMC (used for sample)
Step 2: Backstitch (one strand)		
212		561 Jade-vy. dk. (stems)
382		3371 Black Brown (hangers on ornaments)